Symeon the New Theologian
The Practical and Theological Chapters
Three Theological Discourses

Errata

PAGE	REFERENCE	SHOULD BE
23	St Marinus	St Marina
27	*Ottoban*	*Ottobon*
28	*nous*	*noòs*
40	Mt 5:14	Mt 5:44
56, l.80	*Upostammenos*	*hypotassómenos*
64	word	Word (logos)
84	Lk 6:8	Lk 16:8
103	morning, midday, and evening	evening, morning, and midday

SYMEON THE NEW THEOLOGIAN

THE PRACTICAL AND THEOLOGICAL CHAPTERS

AND

THE THREE THEOLOGICAL DISCOURSES

CISTERCIAN STUDIES SERIES: NUMBER FORTY-ONE

Symeon
THE NEW THEOLOGIAN

THE PRACTICAL AND THEOLOGICAL CHAPTERS

AND

THE THREE THEOLOGICAL DISCOURSES

Translated, with an introduction, by
PAUL McGUCKIN, CP

CISTERCIAN PUBLICATIONS
KALAMAZOO, MICHIGAN
1982

This translation of works by St Symeon the New
Theologian (949-1022) has been made from the edi-
tions of the Greek text prepared by J. Darrouzès in
the series Sources Chrétiennes. The *Chapters* are in
Sources chrétiennes 51 (1957) and the *Discourses* in
Sources chrétiennes 122 (1966).

Symeon the New Theologian
949–1022 A.D.

Reprinted 1994

The work of Cistercian Publications is made possible in part
by support from Western Michigan University to
The Institute of Cistercian Studies

Linotyped at Galesburg, Michigan by Francis Edgecombe   *Printed in the United States of America*

TABLE OF CONTENTS

'He was entirely possessed by the Spirit. His thought was equal to that of the Apostles, for the Divine Spirit inspired his every movement'.*

*Nicetas Stephanos, *Life* 71:31. Cf. *Chapters* 3.77.

THE PRACTICAL AND THEOLOGICAL
CHAPTERS AND THE
THREE THEOLOGICAL DISCOURSES OF
OUR HOLY FATHER
SYMEON THE NEW THEOLOGIAN,
HIGOUMENON OF THE
MONASTERY OF ST MAMAS
OF XEROKERKOS.

INTRODUCTION

b. 949

d. 1022

Our knowledge about Symeon the New[1] Theologian derives primarily from two sources: firstly his own writings, and the clear picture of the theological and psychological persona which emerges from them, and secondly from the account of his life written by his own disciple, Nicetas Stethatos.[2] This biography is the most significant historical source we have, though its authority as a contemporary account has often to be weighed against an awareness of Nicetas' own limitations in aim and and method. In the first place it is written in the manner of byzantine hagiography and, even more, a hagiography very much meant as an *apologia* for a dead master still surrounded, more than a generation after his death, by a certain degree of controversy, if not notoriety. Secondly, Nicetas himself knew Symeon only late in life and only intermittently, for he travelled to see and hear his master in exile, while he himself was a Studite monk at Constantinople. Nicetas freely admits that he uses the testimony and knowledge of other of Symeon's disciples in his construction of the biography. But as Hausherr point out,[3] the earliest date possible for the composition of the work is AD 1052, when the saint's body was brought back to the imperial city. This was thirty years after Symeon's death.

Apart from being his disciple and biographer, Nicetas was also the first editor of the works after Symeon himself.[4] The

1. A title of eminence associating him with John the Theologian, or more probably Gregory the Theologian, i.e. Gregory Nazianzen.

2. Ed. I. Hausherr and G. Horn, *Un Grand Mystique Byzantin: La Vie de S. Symeon Le Nouveau Théologien par Nicetas Stethatos*; Orientalia Christiana 12 (Rome, 1928). Hereafter cited as *Life*.

3. *Life*, p. 17.   4. *Life*, p. 132.

saint had chosen the young monk personally, 'in the hope
that through him all men might make his acquaintance.'[4] This
fact of two editorial hands operating at such an early date
perhaps accounts for the singular disunity of the subsequent
manuscript tradition of the works.

The biography, then, can be expected to be fundamentally
reliable—indeed there is not much else against which we can
measure it—but not above correction in all its details.

Symeon was born some time in AD 949. His baptismal
name was probably George[5] but he adopted a new patronal
saint according to monastic custom. His parents were well-
to-do members of the provincial aristocracy, living at Galatai
in Paphlagonia. Nicetas records that they brought the child
when he was about eleven years old to Constantinople, and
arranged for his education[6] in the household of his uncle,[7]
who was an official of the Imperial Court: 'most likely an
uncle on his father's side under the emperor Romanus Le-
capenus II.'[8] His new patron soon tried to introduce Symeon
to the Emperor and inaugurate a political career for him, but
the boy apparently resisted the idea. We are told that the
uncle died suddenly in 963. It is the same year that Romanus
the Second met his premature end. The political situation in
Byzantium then entered one of its most involved periods,
with the alluring figure of the Empress Theophano, only
twenty-two years old, at the centre of a web of intrigue.[9]
Once the eunuch administration had been overthrown, she

5. This is the name he gives to the character in his account of the
first vision he experienced. Cf. the paraphrastic version in Migne,
PG 120:693, and *Catecheses* 22. See Krivocheine's Introduction to
SCh. 96, p. 18.

6. Nicetas calls him *agrammatos*; see SCh. 122, 23.

7. Not his 'grandparents' as it could be read.

8. J. Gouillard: *Dictionnaire de Théologie Catholique.* (E. Amann, ed.) vol. 14, pt. 2. (Paris, 1941), col. 2941.

9. Theophano married Nicephoras Phocas, the ascetic general, and
arranged for his murder by John Zimisces, who in turn mounted the
throne, betrayed Theophano and imprisoned her in a convent.

and Nicephorus Phocas mounted the throne to rule during the minority of her children, Basil[10] and Constantine. Whatever the reasons that prompted Symeon, whether purely personal[11] or political, the boy seems to have taken refuge immediately in the Studite monastery in Constantinople. It was only a temporary stay, but here he first encountered Symeon Eulabes[12] who was to become his spiritual father and the most significant individual influence on his theological and spiritual life. The younger Symeon was still only fourteen years of age. If a monastic vocation was not already there, Eulabes undoubtedly inspired it. The boy returned from the monastery to live with another noble family in the city. This time he did enter the imperial service, eventually assuming the rank of senator, and holding the office of Master of Cape and Sword.[13]

During this time he continued to visit the Studite monastery to see the elder Symeon, who encouraged his spiritual development and introduced him to the writings of Mark the Hermit[14] and Diadochus of Photice. Nicetas tells us that he also became familiar with the works of John Climacus.[15]

About the year 970, twelve months after the murder of Nicephorus, Symeon, then in his early twenties, describes his first vision.[16] Others were to follow.[17] And in 976, the year

10. Later to become Basil II the Bulgarocrator.

11. Symeon seems to have had no real love for his political career; his reminiscences are sometimes disparaging. See Eucharastic Prayers, 2.6-35. (*Catecheses*. Vol. 3.) SCh 113, and Krivocheine; SCh 96, p. 18.

12. Symeon 'The Pious'.

13. Spathocubiculary.

14. An ascetic writer of the fifth century. His treatise on *The Spiritual* Law is found in PG 65:905-29. G. Maloney's book *Russian Hesychasm* (The Hague, 1973), 78-102, illustrates how much of Symeon's ascetical doctrine is dependent on earlier patristic sources.

15. PG 120:617A.

16. (Paraphrastic version) PG 120:693. *Life*, pp. 57f, and *Catecheses* 22.88-104; SCh 104.

17. See the classic account of his vision of Divine Light: *Hymns* 25.

of John Zimisces death, and the accession of Basil II to his
own government, Symeon Eulabes arranged for our Symeon
to enter the monastery of Stoudios. He left Constantinople
at this time for a final visit in Paphlagonia to his family, to set-
tle his affairs, and to say his farewells. He entered the Studite
community in Byzantium in 977, and the *higoumenon*[18] Peter
placed him under the care and direction of Symeon Eulabes.
For the space of a year they lived in the same cell. He followed a life of constant prayer, strict asceticism, and total
obedience to the elder monk. All that he insists on in his later
writings about spiritual initiation and total submission to the
spritual father was learned at this time. The exceptional pattern of this spirituality, however, seems to have drawn the
attention of the Studite authorities, who judged it as ill-fitting
to the monastic tradition of that house; after only twelve
months, the novice was apparently asked to leave.

Symeon Eulabes took him to the monastery of St Mamas,[19]
where the *higoumenon* Antony accepted him, and within
that year, had him tonsured and professed. The monastery
had been founded under the Emperor Maurice,[20] and according to Nicetas was in some state of disrepair, physically and
morally.[21] Symeon's aristocratic origins, and not least his
noted fervour, ensured that he would soon find preëminence.
Symeon Eulabes probably chose this monastery for his disciple in order to afford him the liberty such a singular spirit
would need. St Mamas was also the patron of Paphlagonia

18. A monastic superior or abbot.

19. St Mamas Megalomartyr of Xerkerkos, celebrated in the Latin
martyrology on 17 August, in the Greek *Menologion* on 2 Septem-
ber. The monastery lay to the west of Byzantium. See Krivocheine's
notes to his Introduction to the *Catechesis*; SCh 96:32.

20. Maurice was assassinated by his general, Phocas, in AD 602.
Pontanus, in his introduction to the works of Symeon preserved in
Migne (PG 120:318), attributes the monastery's foundation to one
Pharasmanes, a Prefect of Chamber under Justinian.

21. *Life* 34.2-6. He says: 'It was no longer a refuge or sheepfold
for monks, but had become a rendezvous for worldly men'.

and greatly revered in Symeon's home region. We could even presume that the *higoumenon* was also a personal friend of Eulabes. It is not surprising then that even by AD 980 Antony presented him to the Patriarch Nicolas Chrysoberges, who ordained him priest.[22]

Antony's death followed soon after and Symeon was elected as the new *higoumenon* and confirmed in office by the Patriarch.[23] He was to remain in this capacity for the next twenty-five years of his life.[24]

Nicetas characterises Symeon at this time as the ideal monastic administrator, rebuilding the Church and repairing the ruined buildings of the complex.[25] What is certain is that his zeal extended to the reform of the common life within his house. His character was forceful and inspired, and his restoration of discipline undoubtedly contributed to make him many enemies among the less enthusiastic members of the community.

He spent the early years of his higoumenate continuing this programme of reform: writing, preaching, and composing a number of hymns. Nicetas tells us that this was a veritable golden age for the St Mamas monastery. It was transformed into a centre of spirituality that attracted the 'entire city', and numbers of young men attached themselves to him as disciples who remained faithful to him even into exile.[26] The only discordant note during this first period of administration came many years later, with a revolt by some thirty of his monks, sometime between 996 and 998. Nicetas describes how several of the community rose up during one of

22. Nicetas says Symeon was a priest for forty-eight years. Hausherr corrects this, as Chrysoberges was elected in 979. J. Gouillard (DTC) suggests an amendment to thirty-eight years of priesthood.
23. *Life* 30.3-5.
24. *Life* 39 and 68.
25. *Life* 34.12-22. Nothing today remains except some marble columns around the Church of Our Lady of Belgrade.
26. *Life* 38.1-2, 44.14-20, and 59.1-4.

his discourses in the monastery church and tried to do physical violence to him there and then.[27] Symeon sat calmly and simply smiled at them, which apparently unnerved them all, for they vented their rage instead on the church windows, and went off *en masse* to the palace of the Patriarch to lodge their case against their *higoumenon*. These kinds of tension are frequently reflected in the writings of Symeon, when he complains bitterly about the numbers of cynical and disillusioned monks that infest any community.[28] Order was soon re-established when the Patriarch Sisinnius judged the case in favour of Symeon and sent the rebellious monks into exile.[29]

Some time between 986 and 987 Symeon Eulabes had died in the Studite monastery. From that time onwards Symeon began that cult of his old master which was eventually to be taken as grounds for his ecclesiastical disgrace. He had an ikon of the Studite painted and set up within the Church of St Mamas. He wrote the *Life* of his spiritual father, composed *Kontakia* in his honour, and instituted a yearly feast and office. To all effects he had canonised Symeon Eulabes and inaugurated a public cult without the Patriarch's authorisation. His behaviour in this matter cannot have been extraordinarily singular, however, for the cult continued in the very heart of the imperial city without interruption for sixteen years.

Nicetas understood, or at least presented, this question of the cult as the sole ecclesiastical grounds for Symeon's trial before the Holy Synod in 1009, though he undoubtedly did this for apologetic reasons, in order to remove any suspicion of contentiousness from his master's behaviour. He presents him above all as a defender of the cult of the saints in the manner of the great monks of previous generations who had suffered prison and tortures in defence of the holy images.[30]

27. *Life* 38.7-10.
28. Cf. *Chapters* 1.22, 1.44, *Catecheses* 3.44-57, and 3.68-77.
29. *Life* 39.6-11.
30. See Leo Allatius, *Notitia*; Migne, PG 120:311f. Symeon is de-

It was an easy matter to describe the Synod's refusal to allow the ikon of Symeon Eulabes in the monastery church in iconoclastic terms, and this probably accounts for the *Menologion*'s[31] description of Symeon's imprisonment: 'Gregorios Decapolitanos discovered Symeon the confessor and godbearer locked in prison on account of the holy images'.

So although the question of the cult itself was not really in issue, it was an emotive symbol of all that had involved Symeon in his conflict with the patriarchal circle. Hausherr describes the cult as 'the primary representative and symbol of the whole theory'.[32] And in times of conflict, any deviation from canonical discipline was likely to be seized on and laid to account by his adversaries.

The conflict with the ecclesiastical authorities seems to have begun in 1003. The main figure in this clash was Stephen, the Metropolitan of Nicomedia, who had resigned his see to become the *synkellos*[33] to the new Patriarch, Sergius. In Nicetas' biography, Stephen is the villain of the piece. He says that the former bishop was consumed with jealousy towards Symeon on account of his eminence in the city as a spiritual teacher[34] and theological writer. He also tells us that Stephen could not forgive Symeon for censuring him in a theological debate on the Trinity. This may well be reflected in the argument of the *First Theological Discourse*. The opponent attacked there is a simple monk however, and Symeon's terms are disparaging in the extreme. Whoever the man is, he is assessed as a 'rash and presumptuous soul', and a 'sense-

scribed as a new Athanasius, Chrysostom, or Theodore Studite, but Allatius gives the reason for his fall not as the images, but as his castigation of the Emperor's loose morals.

31. For 20 November; cf. J. Montanus. *Praefatio*; Migne PG 120: 318f.

32. *Life, Introduction.*

33. Literally, 'in the cell with'. An early form of chaperone for a bishop, this eventually came to be an administrative position.

34. Many eminent men became his disciples: *Life* 54.5, 55.1-2, 104.2-5.

less theologian' destined for God's judgement. Yet it is not too difficult to recognise the figure of the *synkellos* here. His departure from Nicomedia was undoubtedly an attempt to rise higher in the ecclesiastical order, and if there was one thing Symeon could not tolerate, it was the career-cleric. The *synkellos* of the capital undoubtedly carried more weight than a provincial bishop, and had moreover a strong claim on the patriarchal succession. But this was an imperial appointment, and when he resigned his see in order to assume it, Stephen technically lost his former ecclesiastical position and reverted to the monastic condition.[35] This is perhaps why Symeon addresses him as a simple monk. This alone would have been a bitter pill for the ambitious Stephen. It was undoubtedly a stroke of high irony on the part of Symeon in the midst of what he himself saw as an episode in the long-standing conflict between pneumatic monachism and hierarchical authority.

Nicetas accuses Stephen of masterminding the entire attack on Symeon and excessively influencing all the other judges. But the reality of the matter would appear to be a little more complex. Hausherr argues that the conflict was primarily doctrinal,[36] and Darrouzès[37] rightly points out that Stephen was the *synkellos-didaskalos*, and as such fulfilled the role of catechetical administrator and theological advisor to the Patriarch. This role gave him access to the Holy Synod and accounts for his immediate involvement in the case of Symeon.

The issues in the conflict represent old monastic and hierarchic tension, but they can be reduced doctrinally to the following main headings, as far as his trial is concerned:

In the first place there was Symeon's understanding of ecclesiastical discipline. His teaching was quite simple on the

35. See R. Gouillard, 'La collation et la perte des titres nobiliaires à Byzance', *Revue des études byzantines* 4 (1946) 56-69.
36. *Life*, p. 63.
37. *Theological Discourses*, Introduction; SCh 122, 11-12.

point, but extremely radical: authority in the church is pre-eminently the possession of 'the spirituals.' Orders themselves, without the presence of the Spirit witnessed in spiritual charisms and personal holiness, carry no force. It is a little reminiscent of the issues involved in the ancient conflict between Cyprian and the Confessors after the Decian persecution. The stance is perhaps epitomised in Symeon's doctrine of confession. Within the monastic tradition, it was a venerable and longstanding custom to confess to the spiritual elder, whether he was in priestly orders or not.[38] And we can remember that all Symeon's own experience of penance had been with his own master, Symeon Eulabes, who had never been ordained. Symeon then does not invent the position by any means, but as with the question of the cult, he brings it out into the open and makes a theological polemic out of it.[39] His theory of the transmission of this charism to absolve is highly illuminating in this regard. His letter *On those who have power to bind or remit sins*[40] argues that this grace was first given as the *proprium* of the bishops, who lost it through their unworthiness. Then it was passed to the priesthood, who also lost it for the same reason, whereupon it finally came to be the heritage of the monks. The right to absolve is proved and demonstrated by personal holiness and spiritual charisms. The simple fact of possessing the sacrament of orders is not solely to be relied on, for Symeon, and he insists on the necessity of a constant personal union with the divine Spirit, witnessed in visible charisms, to validate and confirm the ministerial functions.[41] Such formulations could only alarm the

38. See S. Vailhe, 'S. Barsanuphe', *Echos D'Orient.* 8 (1905) 20.

39. See *Epistola de confessione*; PG 95:283-304 (under John Damascene but from the hand of Symeon).

40. See K. Holl, *Enthusiasmus und Bussgewalt beim griechischen Mönchtum* (Leipzig, 1898) 110ff.

41. Symeon's doctrine on this point demands a very sensitive interpretation. He does not intend to resurrect the Montanist theory that the personal holiness of the minister is necessary for the validity of a

ecclesiastical authorities. The very basis of their own position was threatened, but more seriously, so was the entire question of the Spirit's validation of the church's ministry.[42] This aspect of Symeon's doctrine distinctly opposes the spiritual tradition of the Pseudo-Areopagite,[43] though even Dionysius, who insists that only the priest is allowed by God to absolve, follows the opinion of Origen and doubts whether a sinful minister could 'give light' to anyone or act as a channel of grace.[44]

The other major doctrinal area for the Synod was Symeon's descriptions of baptism, and the 'second baptism' of the Spirit.[45] For Symeon, the evangelical tradition is far from being a deposit of intellectually appreciable facts that can be reduced to propositional form and consequently handed down through history in a mechanical, repetitious fashion. He constantly insists that it is a supremely personal mystery, a question of Christ's presence to his Church in the Spirit. The dogmatic tradition is one and the same as the sacrament of the Church's holiness and its union with its Head and Lord.[46] And this is why he wishes to make a strong distinction between the simple act of administering the sacrament of baptism and the real conversion and commitment to Christ, of which this is the symbol, but not always the ever present

---

sacrament, and his major point, that non-ordained monks can validly absolve, has a long-standing patristic tradition to support it (see K. Holl, *Enthusiasmus und Bussgewalt*, 138-233). For a brief analysis of Symeon's overall position see G. Maloney, *The Mystic of Fire and Light* (New Jersey) 1975, 169-176.

42. See J. Darrouzès, introduction to the *Theological Discourses*, SCh 122, 32f; and also A. Kambylis, introduction to the *Hymnen*, *Studia Byzantina* 3 (New York) 1976, xvi, fn. 6.

43. See Ps. Dionysius, *Epistola* 8; *Ad monachum Demophilum*; PG 3:1083f. See also, O. Bardenhewer, *Patrology* (St. Louis, 1908) 585f, and B. Altaner, *Patrology* (London, 1960) 639.

44. See Altaner, *Patrology*, 609.

45. See *Chapters* 1.35-36. Perhaps the clearest statement of his position occurs in *Chapters* 3.45.

46. See *Chapters* 3.4.

reality. For Symeon, the possession of the Spirit must always be a reality that is intuitively experienced by the Christian.[47] To be unsure of whether we have the Spirit, or not to know, is for him simply not to have it.[48] Against this, the *synkellos* and the patriarchal circle were equally determined to insist on the inevitable consecratory effect of baptism, whether or not the neophyte showed subsequent signs of the spiritual charisms. The patriarchal theologians were unwilling to allow that the immediate, personal experience of the Spirit's illumination was the only justification for assuming the role of theological teacher, and the sole factor that validated the teacher's statements. For Symeon it was an obvious fact, and central to his whole concept of divine relevation. On this matter, his thought is perhaps most clearly expressed within the present writings in the analogy of the tradition as a chain of gold, whose links are individual saints reaching back in a line of unbroken inspiration to Christ, who gave the Spirit to the Church.[49]

The heart of the controversy was really hermeneutical, a matter of theological emphases and formulation. This was probably recognised at the time by the Patriarch, and this accounts for Symeon's condemnation on the basis of the cult

47. Symeon taught, in regard to baptism, that some real experience of conversion was demanded: 'unless the soul knowingly receives the Kingdom of God, in a manner intelligible to the senses, which it can feel, then the hope of salvation is rendered futile.' (*Oratio* 13; PG 120:379A). See also *Life* 73, where Nicetas reports him as saying that 'not all the baptised accept Christ through their baptism, but only those who are confirmed in faith and have a full knowledge and have passed through their purification.'

48. The adjective *Aisthētos* is very important for him in this sense. It reappears often in the *Chapters*. Symeon has been wrongly accused of Messalianism over this. He is not materialising God but insisting that our experience of God must be a real one. See J. Darrouzès, 'Notes sur les homelies Ps. Macaire', *Muséon* 67 (1954) 307. In this, Symeon is faithfully following the Evagrian tradition of mysticism. See V. Lossky, *The Vision of God* (London: Faith Press, 1973) 85-94. Cf. *Chapters* 1.7, 3.47, 3.58, and 3.100.

49. See *Chapters* 3.4.

of Symeon Eulabes rather than on the much more serious charge of heresy. Even within one year, the Patriarch was ready to rehabilitate him, though the exercise of his condemnation undoubtedly seemed most necessary in order to assert the supremacy of the episcopal teaching authority over the tradition of sophic illumination. The conflict, then, was a clash of two basic attitudes within the Church and the theological tradition; one was the mystical train, emphasising the fundamental importance of union with God and illumination from on high before one begins to speak about the things of God. It recalls to the mind of the Church that theology is a matter not of propositions, but of persons, and ultimately not dogmas, but union with the person of Christ himself.[50] The other attitude was the rational and authoritative analysis which saw its role as the conservative defender of truth by preservation, and which fostered the rational sytematisation of the deposit of dogma. Symeon would not even allow that a theological tradition is possible, unless it is inaugurated and governed by the experience of the Holy Spirit illuminating the mind of the believer. He says that without this experience people can only repeat meaningless formulas they will never understand.[51]

Nicetas tells us that the conflict with the *synkellos* had begun in 1003. Within the space of two years Symeon was forced to resign his position as *higoumenon* at St Mamas, and his disciple Arsenius took his place. He spent the next four years in the monastery, devoting himself to a further campaign of writing. To this period we can almost certainly date his *First Apology* and certain apologetic writings to the *synkellos*.

50. Union with Christ is the climax of the spiritual life in Symeon's teaching. His theology is profoundly christocentric, and he believed one experiences the divine light solely for the purpose of this union. See his *Eucharistic Prayers* 1; SCh 113:156ff, and *Catecheses*; SCh 96: 26ff.
51. *Chapters* 1.41.

At the end of 1008 he was summoned for trial before the Holy Synod in Byzantium. The main charge brought against him was the unofficial cult he had celebrated for Symeon Eulabes, but aspects of his theological teachings were also questioned, and he was formally condemned by the bishops. The ikon of Eulabes was ordered to be removed from the monastery church, and on the third of January 1009, Symeon was sent into exile. Several of his disciples chose to accompany him. They landed at Chrysopolis[52] on the Asiatic coast of the Bosphorus and settled nearby at the small village of Paloukiton. Here there was a small deserted oratory dedicated to St Marinus. They repaired it and lived as a small religious foundation. Symeon's fame as a *thaumaturgos* and spiritual teacher continued to attract disciples and visitors to his place of exile, as indeed it would continue to do until his death.

With the continuing support of his friends and disciples who remained in Constantinople, he was able to submit a *Second Apology*, which was read before the Patriarch[53] and effected his rehabilitation. It seems that Sergius offered to restore him to his position at St Mamas, and was even willing to allow him a discreet cult of Symeon Eulabes. He was consoled with the promise of episcopal consecration within a short time.[54]

It would have been most unlike Symeon to accept any ecclesiastical preferment that was offered to him as 'compensation', and in any case it seems that his experience of life in exile, with his closest disciples, was much more pleasurable and preferable to a return to the city. He declined all offers, and rebuilt the ruins at Paloukiton into a new monastery where he lived with his disciples for the last twelve years of his life. In this last period of his life he composed the magnifi-

---

52. Now known as Scutari. 53. *Life*, pp. 140–2.

54. See Gouillard, *DTC* 14/2:2944, and *Life* 103, 106: pp. 142–6. J. Darrouzès, *Introduction to Theological Discourses*, SCh 122, 33.

cent *Hymns*[55] which stand at the zenith of byzantine mystical writing.

On 12 March 1022 he died, at the age of 73, from an attack of dysentery. His relics were brought back in ceremony to Constantinople in 1052.

And yet the controversy surrounding his life and work seems to have continued. All the relevant writings of Nicetas, who composed the *Life* and an edition of the *Hymns* at this time[56] are notably apologetic and defensive in tone. Symeon's reputation as saint and mystic nevertheless spread. And within a hundred years his own cult, which had been localised in Byzantium, was observed universally in the Orthodox Church.

Symeon's greatest number of disciples undoubtedly came after his death. He had been the champion of the monks, and it is not surprising that we should find the monks championing his theology. His writings on prayer ensured his popularity as a mystical theologian, especially on Mount Athos,[57] and so it was that his work became perhaps the most important influence over the rise and development of the hesychast movement. He was also the inspiration behind Cabasilas' *Life in Christ*, as well as the work of Gregory Palamas.

It is important to remember that Symeon was two centuries removed from hesychasm as we have come to know it, and he cannot be simply identified as a 'hesychast' theologian without more ado.[58] Nonetheless almost all the major themes of the later hesychasts can be discovered in his writings: the manner of meditation, the transfiguration of the new man, the transforming energies of the Spirit, and the vision of the uncreated Light. The similarity is so striking that in his study

55. *Life*, p. 145.   56. See PG 120:310.

57. See the account given by L. Allatius in the seventeenth century: PG 120:311.

58. See B. Krivocheine, *Introduction* to the *Catecheses*; SCh 96, 54, note 1.

of the saint, Holl says: 'In all its major lineaments the hesychast tradition is really a recapitulation of the thought of Symeon.'[59] Symeon was undoubtedly the supreme inspiration widely read on Athos. One notable exception is that he never mentions the *Jesus Prayer*.

Symeon's spiritual doctrine represents a synthesis of two major types of ascetic approach, the Alexandrian or Sinaitic tradition, and the Macarian school.[60] The dominant theme of the former was the blessedness of the pure heart which 'sees' God;[61] that of the latter is what Hausherr calls the tradition 'of the intimation or of the gift of supernatural knowledge,'[62] represented especially in the writings of Diadochus of Photike as well as those of Macarius.[63]

Meyendorff sees the role of Symeon in terms of a synthesis of two equally popular monastic traditions: that of John Climacus and Theodore Studite, and he points out that Symeon was particularly remarkable in the way he transformed the Evagrian tradition of *hesychia*,[64] with its insistence on absolute solitude[65] remote from the affairs of men,[66] and practised it in a Studite monastery in the very heart of Constantinople.[67]

Symeon's final role in the development of hesychast theology is reached only when we come to Gregory Palamas, the great theologian whose task it was to defend the orthodoxy of the hesychast monks. His own work was a theological

59. K. Holl. *Enthusiasmus*, p. 215.

60. Hausherr: *Les grands courants de la spiritualité orientale; Orientalis Christiana Periodica*. 1. (1935) 126f; See also Krivocheine, *Catecheses*; SCh 96, p. 39, note 3.

61. See *Chapters* 3.29–32, 3.35.

62. See Hausherr, *Les grands courants*, 126, and also *Chapters* 3.44.

63. See Lossky, *The Vision of God*, 95f.

64. See *Chapters* 1.95.

65. Hausherr, *L'Hesychasme, Orientalis Christiana Periodica* 22 (1956) 8-11, and Lossky, *The Vision of God*, 85–94.

66. This theme is still present in his thought, of course. See *Chapters* 3.86.

67. See Hausherr, *L'Hesychasme*, 260–1.

systematisation which synthesized Symeon's work yet again, and in so doing gave it its final place of honour in the perspectives of Orthodox theology. Meyendorff sums up the terms of this synthesis in the following manner:

> So we find in Palamas, the hesychast doctor, at one and the same time an integration of Evagrian terminology, a theological assimilation of the mysticism of St Symeon the New Theologian, and a justification of the prayer methods of the thirteenth century. In his Christocentricity, his theology of the light, and his eucharistic spirituality[68] Palamas undoubtedly depends on the great mystic of the eleventh century, though he hardly ever refers to him. All the prophetic elements in Symeon and all his personal mysticism are re-expressed by Palamas with a theological rigour that they never had originally.[69]

And Symeon needed such a theological resolution. He always spoke from his own immediate experience,[70] but always more as the spiritual master than the systematic theologian. In his later systematisation of the hesychast tradition, Palamas showed himself to be a true disciple of Symeon, and probably the greatest, for he continued the master's inspiration and brought it to a final perfection.

68. The eucharistic theology of Symeon is not as prevalent in the works translated here as it is in his other works, but the Eucharist symbolises for him the putting on of Christ in light. See PG 120:525D.

69. J. Meyendorff, *Introduction à l'étude de Grégoire Palamas*, p. 221.

70. See *Ethical Discourse* 9 and J. Darrouzès, SCh 122, 23.

The present translation of the *Chapters* has been made from the Greek text of the critical edition prepared by J. Darrouzès in volume 51 of the *Sources Chrétiennes Series* (1957). That of the *Three Theological Discourses* is taken from the text prepared by the same scholar in *Sources Chrétiennes* volume 122 (1966).

THE CHAPTERS

The Chapters are purely monastic in character and are evidently the fruit of Symeon's many instructions to his monks. Darrouzès calls them the most restrained of all his writings[71] and their character as, in part, an initiation into the monastic state may well account for that. Their format represents a certain progress through spiritual degrees: from *praxis* through *gnosis* to *theologeia*, or illumined union with God. The soul moves upwards away from fear into the love of God, and simultaneously progresses through moral fidelity and the *katharsis* of suffering to the enjoyment of the vision of God.

There is no accurate date for the *Chapters*, and indeed the nature of the text makes it evident that they were composed throughout Symeon's long career as a spiritual master. They were probably assembled by Symeon himself, and Darrouzès considers this editorial work was accomplished towards the end of his life.[72]

Although they are not *Centuries* as such, but *Chapters*, the structure is quite clearly that adopted in the critical edition: (100) – (25) – (100). The first series of *Chapters* upsets the rule in that it consists of 101, and appears to have been miscopied at a very early date. There are several places where one can argue that the text has been mistakenly divided: for example, between chapters 51 and 52, or again between 57 and 58. In addition to this, the *Ottoban manuscript* makes

71. *Introduction*, SCh 51, 33.   72. *Ibid.*, p. 36.

Chapters 1.86–7 into one unit, and the *Xenophon manuscript* elides *Chapters* 1.96–7.

Several *Chapters* were added on as accretions over the ages to those originally by Symeon. These can be found in the Migne edition of the texts: PG 120:604ff. Within the primitive manuscript tradition two others were added on to the very end of the third series:

a. *Poion poiou prōton huparchei*: which is a textual gloss. and

b. *Hēsuchia esti nous*: which is from the hand of Stethatos.

Both versions can be found in Darrouzès' Appendix, SCh 51, 115.

THE THREE THEOLOGICAL DISCOURSES

Nicetas Stethatos' *Life* is too vague on the order of Symeon's writings to allow us to date this composition with any precision at all. Together with the *Ethical Discourses*, the work forms a lengthy collection of treatises and was again probably assembled over a space of time. J. Darrouzès postulates a date for the whole collection of somewhere between 1000 and 1009, when Symeon was entering into the period of conflict with the *Synkellos* Stephen.

As he taught in the *Chapters*, the only way to theological truth is held to be spiritual union with God. The only valid thought about God is one that the Spirit himself has inspired and illuminated. The *Three Discourses* are a defence of trinitarian orthodoxy.[73] The first argues for the equality of the hypostases and censures any theologising that is not directly illumined by the Spirit and which does not follow the pattern of Christ's own humility. The second begins with an attack on all false theologians who speak without possessing the Spirit, and then revolves round the theme of the threefold divine image in man, and its implications for trinitarian theol-

73. See K. Holl. *Enthusiasmus*, pp. 104f.

ogy. The third begins with the concept of the divine unity expressed and affirmed in christian prayer and experience, and concludes with a magnificently poetic account of the attributes of God as light.

They appear to have been written at about the same time, and Darrouzès is of the opinion that they were composed together for some kind of scriptural debate in Byzantium centring round the theme of Jn 14:28: 'The Father is greater than I.'[74] The Johannine text most certainly seems to have been the starting point for the whole controversy, though whether the *Treatises* are to be seen in the context of an arranged debate,[75] or in the wider perspective of Symeon's opposition to the *Synkellos*, as Nicetas suggests, is a matter that can no longer be clearly settled.

Symeon is justifiably given the illustrious title of 'the theologian' by the eastern Church and his work deserves to be read widely in the West and pondered deeply by western theologians. His writings not only speak eloquently of the love of Christ but, in addition, we find in him a prophet for our times who points the way forward to the renaissance of modern theological study which so often seems to be trapped between the Scylla of ephemeral trendiness and the Charybdis of mindless repetition of antique formulae. The contemporary spirit of critical research, rising from the Enlightenment, has broken the strangle-hold that scholasticism once had on western theologians and theology now has unparalleled opportunities to enquire into the origins of Christianity and the heart of the Christian tradition, that is, trinitarian theology, christology, and soteriology. Our present age, with rich resources at hand, has witnessed something of a resurgence of christological studies, but the great patristic analyses

---

74. SCh 122:14.

75. The reference to 'my opponent' in the opening of the first *Discourse* is a typical apologetic form of the Fathers and does not imply a personal encounter.

of the trinitarian nature of the Œconomy are still a neglected area, and this perhaps suggests that these things are not foremost in the hearts of the faithful, and have passed from being the central pillars of the christian life to become something esoteric and exotic.

Without the perspectives of the Fathers on these lofty theological themes, modern theology runs the risk of being fragmented into a myriad host of different 'theologies'. The return to the Fathers can save the Church from the ultimate sterility of such fragmentation on the one hand, and from a confused dwelling in the past, on the other. Symeon is a perfect starting point for us. In his work we see that profound and overriding conviction that there is, in truth, but one theology, the Church's living tradition, and this as the divine Spirit of life and holiness presenting Christ to each generation and each believer. In Symeon's hands theology and spirituality overcome the disastrous divorce one witnesses all too often, for they both find their atonement in the person of the Divine Wisdom.

This rediscovery of the mind of the Fathers, so beautifully manifested in Symeon the New Theologian, is as pressing for the Church today as ever it was when in the tenth century Symeon wrote these texts.

Paul McGuckin

La Sainte Union College
Southampton

THE PRACTICAL AND THEOLOGICAL CHAPTERS

1.1 WHEN MEN SEARCH FOR GOD with their bodily eyes they can find him nowhere, for he is invisible. But for those who ponder in the Spirit, he is present everywhere. He is in all, yet beyond all. In this, his salvation is near to those who fear him,[1] but far away from sinful men.[2]

1.2. The remembrance of Christ brings light to one's mind and drives away the demons, and the light of the Holy Trinity which shines in a pure heart lifts it away from the whole world. When a man participates in this, though he is still on earth, he has a taste of the glory to come, at least in so far as he can, for although he is moved by heaven's grace he is still wrapped in the veil of flesh.[1]

1.3. If, when all visible reality has passed away, nothing shall exist but God, who is and ever shall be, then those who share in the riches of his grace within this world are already enjoying their riches of the age to come, even though they are still on earth. They groan in the shadows under the weight of their burden.[1]

1.4. Those who simply teach do not gain the Lord's blessing. It is for those who have first practised the commandments and so have deserved to see and contemplate the shining and brilliant radiance of the Spirit within themselves. For with this vision, this knowledge and power, the Spirit instructs them fully in all that they must speak of and teach to others. So, as I have said, all those who try to teach must first of all become students[1] lest they wander off and lose

1.1.[1] Ps 85:9.
1.1.[2] Ps 119:155.
1.2.[1] Heb 10:20.
1.3.[1] I.e., the pain of separation; cf. Rom 8:22.
1.4.[1] Mt 5:19.

themselves by speaking of things outside their experience. This is the fate of men who trust in themselves.

1.5. The man who has no fear of God does not believe either that God exists, for he is a fool.[1] But the man who does believe also fears [God], and, fearing him, keeps his commandments. The man who says he fears God but does not keep his commandments is a liar, and the fear of God is not in him.[2] For it is written: 'Where there is fear, the commandments are kept.'[3] So if the fear of God is not in us and we do not keep the divine commandments, then we are no different from the pagans and the unbelievers.

1.6. Faith, the fear of God, and the observance of his commandments, bring us a reward in proportion to our purity. For as we are purified, so we rise from fearing God to loving him. It is like making progress and passing out of fear into God's love.[1] It is then that we hear: 'He who accepts my commandments and keeps them is the one who loves me.'[2] So then, let us redouble our efforts to prove our love by our works. For when we have done this, he himself loves us just as he promised and his Father loves us in the same way, and the Holy Spirit, of course, comes before him to prepare a dwelling place. So it is that by the indwelling unity of the hypostases, we become the home of the Father, the Son, and the Spirit.

1.7. When the three-personed diety dwells within the saints[1] and is known and felt to be present, it is not the fulfilment of desire, but the cause and beginning of a much greater and fervent desire. Because from this time on, the man who enjoys the presence finds that it gives him no rest. It drives him on towards the flames of an ever deepening desire for the

1.5.[1] Ps 14:1, 53:1.
1.5.[2] 1 Jn 2:4.
1.5.[3] Ps 112:1.

1.6.[1] 1 Jn 4:17-8.
1.6.[2] Jn 14:21.

1.7.[1] *Lit.*: 'in the completed or perfected ones' (*teleiois*), but as his next idea illustrates, this sanctity is not a finished state but a process.

Godhead as if he were being consumed and devoured by fire. The mind can find no limit in the one it yearns for. It cannot grasp him, and it cannot set any limit on its own desire and love. Yet as it strives to grasp and hold on to this endless goal, it feeds within itself a longing that knows no bounds and a love that can never be satisfied.

1.8. When a man has reached this stage he does not imagine that he has found the source of the love and desire of God within himself. On the contrary, he considers that he really does not love God because he cannot embrace the fullness of love. He rates himself, then, as the lowest of all who fear God, and in the depths of his soul reckons that he is unworthy to be saved along with the faithful.

1.9. For the man who believes, all things are possible[1] because: 'Faith is counted as righteousness,'[2] and 'Christ is the end of the Law.'[3] Belief in him justifies and perfects the believer, for belief in Christ is considered to correspond to the works of the law. It is confirmed and witnessed by the evangelical precepts and so earns for the faithful a participation in eternal life, in Christ himself.

1.10. Belief is a matter of dying for Christ and his commandments. It is believing that such a death is life-giving. It is to count poverty as riches, and to consider the lowest humiliation as true honor and nobility. Faith is believing that when one has nothing, one has everything.[1] More than this, it is to possess the incomprehensible riches of the knowledge of Christ[2] and to look upon all visible things as but clay and smoke.

1.11. To have faith in Christ means more than simply despising the delights of this life. It means we should bear all our daily trials that may bring us sorrow, distress, or unhap-

1.9.[1] Mk 9:23.
1.9.[2] Rom 4:9.
1.9.[3] Rom 10:4.

1.10.[1] 2 Cor 6:9-10.
1.10.[2] Eph 3:8.

piness, and bear them patiently for as long as God wishes and until he comes to visit us. For it is said: 'I waited on the Lord and he came to me.'[1]

1.12. Those who honor their parents before the law of God, in any way at all, are devoid of faith in Christ. Indeed their own conscience accuses them, at least if their conscience has managed to survive their infidelity. The sign of those who really believe is that in no way do they ever transgress the law of our great God and of our Saviour Jesus Christ.

1.13. Faith in God engenders the desire for good and the fear of punishment. This desire for better things and the fear of punishment bring about in turn a zealous observance of the commandments; and a zealous observance of the commandments teaches men about their own fragility. The thought of our fragility reminds us of our death, and if a man keeps this thought with him always, how diligently will he search to find out the destiny that awaits him when he departs from this life. But the man who really tries to learn of the things to come must first of all detach himself from present realities. No one can have a perfect knowledge of these matters if he is held back by such an attachment, no matter how small it may be. If a man gains some taste of all this through the divine economy, but even then does not immediately renounce whatever attachment hinders his total surrender to this knowledge, not even admitting voluntarily a single foreign thought, then even that which he thought he had will be taken from him.[1]

1.14. If you renounce the world in a total solitude which tries to set aside all the affairs and manners and opinions and outward appearances[1] of this life, and [if you] deny the body and self-will, then within a short time this becomes a source of great benefit for anyone who makes this renunciation fervently.

1.11.[1] Ps 40:1.   1.13.[1] Mt 13:12.   1.14.[1] *prosopa*.

1.15. If you have fled from the world, make sure you never start allowing your soul the consolation of going back for visits, even if all your family and friends insist that you should. For this is inspired in them by the demons in order to cool the fervor of your heart. Since they cannot frustrate your resolve completely, they will always be trying to make it more slack.

1.16. It is when you seem strong and indifferent in the face of all the charms of life that the demons rouse up the feelings of those close to you and make them wail and lament about you, even in your very presence. You will see the truth of this when you remain steadfast in your resolve, for you will see them suddenly boil with anger and hatred, push you away like an enemy, and no longer want to set eyes on you.

1.17. When you see the distress of your parents and brothers and friends on your account, you must scorn the devil whose trickery has roused up these feelings against you. Go away as quickly as you can with great fear. Pray earnestly to God that you might soon come to the harbor of the good Father where he himself shall give rest to your weary and troubled soul. The ocean of life has many occasions of danger and final ruination.

1.18. If a man wants to hate the world, he must have the love of God in the depths of his soul. He must think of God constantly. There is nothing better than these virtues to make us abandon all things joyfully and cast them away like dross.

1.19. Have no desire to keep the slightest attachment to this world, not even for good motives, for in fact they would only be silly pretences. When you have been called, obey instantly,[1] for nothing pleases God so much as our promptness; 'a poor man's willingness is better than a rich man's sloth.'[2]

1.19.[1] Cf. 1 Kgs 19:19-21.
1.19.[2] This would appear to be a contemporary proverb.

1.20. If the world and all that is in the world is to pass away, and only God is immortal and eternal, then you should rejoice, for on his account you have abandoned corruptible things. Corruptible things are not only riches and possessions, but even every sinful pleasure and enjoyment in corruption. Only the commandments of God are light and life, and all men acknowledge them as such.

1.21. My brother, if you have received the flame and have come eagerly to a monastery or a spiritual father because of it, then even if he or your brethren should advise you to use baths, take food or other bodily comforts that pass as remedies, do not agree with them. Be always ready for fasting, mortification, and strict discipline. If, however, your father in the Lord should command you to enjoy some comfort, then you should obey. Do not follow your own will in these matters. Apart from this, keep to what you yourself chose for the good of your soul and do it joyfully. If you keep to this rule you will always be able to consider yourself an ascetic and disciplined man, one despoiled of self-will in every circumstance. Moreover, you will keep a flame in your heart that never burns out, but urges you on to count all things as nothing.[1]

1.22. When the demons have done all they can, but have been unable to hinder or deflect our divine purpose, they then enter into the pious manner of hypocrites, and through them try to hinder those who are making efforts. First of all, as if love and consideration were really their motives, they advise them to take a rest, saying, 'you should not weaken your bodies or you will fall into listlessness.'[1] Then they invite you to useless gatherings and make you waste entire days in this way. If someone who was once obedient to the fervent

1.21.[1] Cf. Phil 3:8.

1.22.[1] The temptation of *accidia*, physical and spiritual aridity and weariness, attributed by the Fathers to the 'noon-day devil' (see Ps 91:6); cf. *Chapters* 1.71.

ones should imitate them, they soon cast him aside and laugh at his ruination. But if he refuses to agree with what they say and holds aloof from them all, recollected and reserved, then they turn to hatred and will try anything they can to drive him from the monastery. A scorned pride cannot bear to see humility honored before it.

1.23. The proud man frets when he sees the tears[1] of the humble man doubly honored: before God as they move his pity, and in the sight of men as they earn him praise he never sought.

1.24. From the moment you put yourselves completely in the hands of your spiritual father, you should know that you become a stranger to all that leads you outside, I mean the affairs and riches of men. Without his [permission], you should want to have no dealings or business here. You should no longer ask him to leave you anything, great or small, only that which he tells you to take from his own hand. He will act on his own discretion in this.

1.25. Unless your spiritual father allows it, do not give alms from the goods you have brought with you and do not even allow people to use them through your agent. It is better to be poor and a stranger and to have a reputation for this, than to distribute goods and give to the poor while you are still a novice. If you have a pure faith you will abide by the decision of your spiritual father as if everything were in the hands of God.

1.26. Never ask for water to drink even if thirst is burning you up. Wait until your spiritual father decides to offer you a drink. Do violence to yourselves! Overcome in all things! Convince your reason by saying, 'If God wills'. And if you deserve something to drink, he will surely reveal this to your spiritual father and he will say to you, 'drink'. Then you can

1.23.[1] On the gift of tears in the thought of S. Symeon, see B. Krivocheine's Introduction to the *Catecheses*; SCh 96:48-50.

drink with a clear conscience even if it is not the correct time for it.

1.27. A man who had extensive spiritual experience and a pure faith, who trusted in God as the witness of truth, once said: 'I have taken this resolution to heart: "I shall never ask my father for anything to eat or drink and I will never take anything at all independently of him. I will wait until God inspires him and he instructs me." ' And he added: 'In this way I have never fallen away from my goal.'

1.28. When a man has gained a vivid faith in his father under God, whenever he looks at him he thinks he is looking at Christ himself. When he is with this father or following him, he firmly believes that he is with Christ and following him. When he feels this he will never want to associate with anyone else, and nothing in the world will be preferable to the love and memory of him.[1] For what is better or more useful in this life or the next than to be with Christ? What can be more beautiful and delightful than to see him? If a man is favored with his companionship he can truly draw from it eternal life.

1.29. If a man habitually loves and prays for those who injure and treat him unjustly,[1] those who hate him and shun his presence, then he will make great progress in a short time. For when we feel this in our hearts, it plunges all our thought into the abyss of humility and into that spring of tears in which all three parts of the soul are washed.[2] It raises our mind to the heights of impassibility[3] and brings us to contem-

1.28.[1] A reference to Symeon the Pious, the spiritual father of the writer.

1.29.[1] Mt 5:14.

1.29.[2] See *Chapters* 3.63. The byzantine philosophers, following Plato, labelled the three parts of the soul as *epithumētikon* (the desiring part), *thumikon* (the irascible part) and *logistikon* (the rational part). See *Chapters* 3.63 below.

1.29.[3] See B. Krivocheine, *Dans la lumière du Christ* (Chevetôgne, 1979) 375-86, and J. Darrouzès, SCh 122:29-30, for Symeon's doctrine of impassibility.

plation where we find a taste of blessedness. Henceforth it looks down on all the things of this life as mere dross; even food and drink no longer delight and have little attraction.

1.30. It shows that we have a vivid faith when we even take the ground on which our father and guide stands and venerate it as a holy place, or if we fervently take the dust from beneath his feet and sprinkle it over our heads and rub it over our breast as a remedy against the passions and a purification of sins. We should hardly dare to approach him or even touch one of his tunics or habits without his command. If you touch or handle something that belongs to him, do it with fear and respect, telling yourself that you are not worthy to be a servant and look upon these things, not even worthy to go into his cell.

[marginal note: ?? Did Jesus make disciples do this?]

1.31. There are many who renounce this life and the affairs of this life, but few who do so by their own will. The saying of the Lord rightly refers to this when it states: 'Many are called, but few are chosen.'[1]

1.32. When you have sat down to table with all the brothers and everything appears to the eyes of your mind as shadows, and you do not even notice the taste of the food, and your soul is amazed at this marvel, brimming with tears, you should know then that the grace of God has granted you this sign because of the great humility that rises from your fear. So when you see these works of God and realize the feebleness of external experience, then take hold of your fear and graft it onto the love of inner realities. This is that spiritual wisdom you will hear about. It is found midway between fear and love, and it makes men pass from the one to the other without feeling and without danger.

[marginal note: incarnation?]

1.33. There is no other way of gaining and keeping hold of a perfect love for God except to the extent that we have spiritual wisdom, and this increases gradually through the

1.31.[1] Mt 22:14.

daily asceticism of our soul. The apostle knew this when he said, 'We see the Creator by analogy with the greatness and beauty of his creation.'[1]

1.34. No man can use his visual sense alone and properly comprehend the greatness of the heavens or the extent of the earth or the order of all things. How could bodily eyes ever manage to grasp things that transcend mind and understanding? It is only with difficulty that the mind can gain a true contemplation of existing reality, and only then after it has been purified of its own opinions, freed of its prejudices, and illumined by the grace and mercy of God. Even then it only perceives in so far as it has been illuminated.

1.35. During the night our eyes can make out only the spot where we light the glowing lantern. The rest of the world is night for us. In the same way, for those who sleep in the night of sin, the Good Master becomes only a faint glimmer. Even though he is the God who cannot be limited, he is limited by our weakness. But when a man suddenly lifts his eyes and contemplates the nature of reality in a way he has never done before, then he trembles and tears flood out spontaneously though he feels no sorrow. They purify him and wash him in a second baptism, that baptism Our Lord speaks about in the Gospels: 'If a man is not born of water and the Spirit, he will not enter the kingdom of heaven.'[1] And again he says: 'If he is not born from on high.'[2] When he said 'from on high', he signified being born of the Spirit.

1.36. In the first baptism, water symbolizes tears and the oil of chrismation prefigures the inner anointing of the Spirit. But the second baptism is no longer a type of the truth, but the truth itself.[1]

1.33.[1] Cf. Rom 1:20.
1.35.[1] Jn 3:5.
1.35.[2] As in the Greek text of John, the word *anōthen* has the double sense of 'a second time' and 'from above'.
1.36.[1] For Symeon's doctrine of the second baptism, see B. Krivocheine, *Dans la lumière du Christ*, 148-55.

1.37. It is not enough simply to abstain from evil deeds, the ascetic must strive to be free of contrary thoughts and imaginations and to be constantly engaged in spiritual meditations for the good of his soul. This is how he will remain free from the cares of life.

1.38. A man can lay bare his whole body, but if he keeps a veil over his eyes and refuses either to lift it up or take it away, then the nakedness of the rest of his body will not enable him to see the light. It is the same with a man who has scorned all other affairs or riches and broken all attachment to them; if he does not free the eye of the soul from the pre-occupations of life or from evil thoughts, then he shall never see our Lord and God, Jesus Christ himself, the intelligible light.

1.39. Worldly thoughts and the cares of life have the same effect on the understanding as a veil draped over the eyes, for the understanding is the eye of the soul. So long as we leave them there, we cannot see. But when they fall away as we remember that we are to die, then we shall clearly see the true light which illumines every man as it comes into the world from on high.[1]

1.40. A man who is blind from birth will neither understand nor believe the significance of what is written here. But when a man has been judged worthy to see, then he will bear witness that what we say is true.

1.41. When a man can see with his eyes, he knows when it is night and when it is day. But a blind man is unaware of both. And when a man looks upward through the Spirit and sees through the eyes of the mind, he contemplates the true and inaccessible light. So if he then falls back into his former blindness through carelessness and is deprived of the light, he will really suffer the loss and know the reason for it all too

1.39.[1] Jn 1:9.

well. But the man who is blind from birth[1] knows nothing of these things either from experience or his efforts, unless perhaps he catches something from hearsay and so learns about things he has never seen. Such a man may tell others what he has heard, but neither he nor his audience will know what they are talking about.[2]

1.42. It is impossible to stuff your body to the limit with food and enjoy spiritually the intelligible consolation of God. You move away from it the more you look after your belly. So the more roughly you treat your body, the more will you be filled with spiritual food and comfort.

1.43. We should not renounce just riches or gold or the other things of life; we ought to renounce all earthly things. We should even root out from our soul the desire that tends towards them. Let us not only rate the pleasures of the body and all their irrational tendencies, but also strive to mortify it with trials. It is the cause of our desires being roused and stirred into action, and as long as it lives, our soul is necessarily dead. Even when it is not opposed, it is hardly disposed, to all the commandments of God.

1.44. The flame of a fire always reaches upwards, even if you turn the lighted stick upside down. And in the same way the heart of the proud man is incapable of humility. The more you give him suitable advice, the more he elevates himself. If you admonish or rebuke him he answers back aggressively, but if you praise or encourage him he is shamefully puffed up.

1.45. The man who has the habit of contradicting things

1.41.[1] Symeon intends here to arouse overtones of the Johannine faith-light theme: cf. Jn 9. The Johannine flavor of this passage continues from his citation of John at *Chapters* 1:39, and his allusion to the Johannine 'witness' theme at *Chapters* 1:40.

1.41.[2] He implies that theology is ultimately a personal reality, an illumination personally communicated by the Spirit and prepared for by total submission to one's spiritual master.

becomes a two-edged sword for himself. He destroys his own soul without knowing it, and estranges it from eternal life.

1.46. Someone who likes contradicting is like a man who freely surrenders himself to the enemies ranged against his emperor. The spirit of contradiction is a snare which uses self-justification as its bait, and it is by this means that we are deceived into swallowing the fishhook of sin. Then, taken by tongue and mouth, the poor soul becomes the prey of the spirits of evil. They either carry it up to the heights of pride or else cast it down into the chaos of the abyss of sin to be judged along with those who fell from heaven.

1.47. If your heart is inordinately distressed by insults and injuries, you must recognize the sign that you still carry the ancient serpent in your heart. If, then, a man keeps silent or answers back with great humility, he weakens the serpent and breaks its grip. But if he replies with bitterness or speaks arrogantly, he gives the serpent the power to pour its venom into his heart and gnaw him cruelly inside. In this way the serpent grows stronger day by day, and each time the man tries to put things right it devours all the strength of his poor soul. After that he can live only for sin, and is altogether dead to righteousness.

1.48. If you want to renounce the world and be instructed in the evangelical way of life, then do not surrender yourself to a master without experience, or to one still subject to the passions, because he might initiate you into the diabolical life instead of the evangelical. Good masters give good doctrine, but the evil teach evil. Bad seeds always produce rotten fruit.

1.49. Call on God with prayers and tears to send you a holy guide who has overcome the passions.[1] For yourself you should search the divine writings, especially the ascetical

1.49.[1] Impassibility is the mark of the new man, the saint who lives completely in the Spirit and who alone is qualified to speak of that Spirit.

works of the holy fathers.② If you compare these with the
teachings of your own tutor and master, you will be able to
see and learn all these things as if in a mirror. ʃWhatever is in
agreement with the sacred writings hold to your heart and
keep in your thoughts, but discern whatever elements are different or adulterated and cast them away so that you will not
be led astray.ʃ You must understand that there are all too
many deceivers and false teachers these days.

1.50. A deceiver is a man who is blind himself, but who
still tries to guide other people. He leads all who follow him
to their ruination in a ditch, just as the Lord said: 'If the
blind leads the blind, both will fall into the pit.'[1]

1.51. He who is blind before the One is absolutely blind
before all things, but he who sees in the One is in the contemplation of all things. He abstains from the contemplation of
all things and enters into the contemplation of all things, and
is outside all that can be contemplated. Being within the One
such a man sees all things, and being within all things sees
nothing of any of them.

1.52. A man who sees in the One is able, through the One,
to see himself, all men, and all reality, and being hidden within him, sees nothing of all things.

1.53. If a man cannot feel intuitively[1] that he has put on
the image[2] of our heavenly Lord Jesus Christ, man and God,
over his rational and intellectual nature, then he remains but
flesh and blood. He cannot gain an experience of spiritual
glory by means of his reason, just as men who are blind from
birth cannot know sunlight by reason alone.

1.54. The man who sees and hears and experiences in this
way will know what I am talking about, for he already bears

1.49.② The Fathers, as representatives of this 'new man', are thereby inspired by the Spirit. Cf. *Chapters* 1:85, and 2:20-1.
    1.50.[1] Mt 15:14.   1.53.[2] 1 Cor 15:49.
    1.53.[1] *Euaisthētōs kai gnōstōs.*

the image of the heavenly man[1] and has achieved the perfect *individual ?* manhood of the fullness of Christ.[2] In this state, he can lead the flock of Christ properly along the way of God's commandments. But the man who has not learned this, and is different, has obviously not opened the faculties of his soul or made them receptive. It would be much better for him to be led, rather than to lead others precariously.

1.55. When a man regards his guide and teacher as God *149?* himself, he can no longer contradict. If he thinks or claims that he can have both attitudes, he is very mistaken, and does not know how those of God dispose themselves before God.

1.56. Someone who believes that his life and death lie in the hands of his pastor would never contradict him. It is when he is ignorant of this that contentiousness is born, and this is the agent of the mind's eternal death.

1.57. Before he receives the sentence, an accused man has a chance to present a defense of his behavior directly to the judge. But once the facts have been set out and the judge has given his verdict, then there is nothing you can say, great or small, to the executioners.

1.58. So before the monk comes into this tribunal and before he reveals the secrets of his heart, it is perhaps understandable that he should justify himself, either through ignorance or because he thinks he can cover things up. But once he has revealed his thoughts and sincerely confessed, it is no longer right for him to justify himself before his judge after God and his master until death. From the moment a monk goes into this tribunal to bare the secrets of his heart, he must be convinced from the start that whatever he learns he will always deserve a thousand deaths. And if he truly understands the nature of this mystery, he will believe that his obedience and humility will redeem him from all suffering and punishment.

1.54.[1] 1 Cor 15:49.   1.54.[2] Eph 4:13.

1.59. If a man keeps these things always in his thoughts, his heart will never rebel if he should be warned or corrected or admonished. For when a man falls into such faults – and I mean contentiousness and faithlessness with regard to his spiritual father and teacher – he pitifully throws himself into the snare[1] and abyss of hell, even in this lifetime. He becomes the dwelling place of Satan and all his unclean power. He is a child of infidelity and damnation.[2]

1.60. You, however, are a child of obedience,[1] and so I urge you to think of these things constantly and to strive with great fervor never to fall into these hellish evils we have mentioned. Pray fervently to God each day and say: 'God and Lord of all things, who have power over all life and each soul, you alone can heal me. Listen to the prayer of a wretched man. By the presence of your all-holy Spirit bring death to the serpent coiled in my heart and make it disappear. I am poor and naked, devoid of any virtue, but make me worthy to fall in tears at the feet of my holy father, and make his holy soul bend to compassion and pity for me. Lord, give me that lowliness in my heart and my thoughts that is right for a sinner who has resolved to repent. Never finally abandon a soul that has once surrendered to you, confessed its faith in you, and chosen and prized you before the whole world. For you know, Lord, that I wish to be saved in spite of all the evil habits that still fetter me. For you, Master, all things are possible which are impossible to men.'[2]

1.61. Those who, in fear and trembling, have laid the good foundation stone of faith and hope in the hall of righteousness, who have planted their feet[1] immovably on the rock of obedience to their spiritual father, who listen to his teachings as if they came from the mouth of God, those who with humble souls raise an unshakable edifice on this foundation

1.59.[1] Prov 9:18.   1.60.[2] Mk 10:27.
1.59.[2] Eph 2:2, Jn 17:12.   1.61.[1] Prov 3:26.
1.60.[1] Cf. 1 Pet 1:14.

of obedience, these will succeed immediately. It is they who succeed in that basic and all-important goal of self-renunciation. To do another's will instead of one's own leads not only to a denial of one's own life, but even makes a man dead to the entire world.²|

1.62. A man who contradicts his |spiritual| father makes the devils rejoice, but when a man humbles himself even to death, he makes the angels stand amazed. For this man performs the work of God by imitating the Son of God who was perfect in obedience to his own father, even to death, death on a cross.¹

1.63. The untimely throng of the heart's emotions darkens and troubles our thought. It obliterates humility and pure prayer from the soul and brings weariness of heart. This leads to endless aridity and obduracy. It is how the demons try to make spiritual men despair.

1.64. When these troubles affect you, monk, though you can still find zeal within your soul and so great a thirst for perfection that you long to fulfill every commandment of God, even down to avoiding the sin of an idle word,¹ and want to equal the saints of old in virtue, wisdom, and contemplation; or when you see that someone is stopping you from climbing to the heights of holiness by secretly sowing weeds of discouragement,² swaying your thoughts with his comments that 'it is impossible for you to be saved in the midst of this world, or even to keep the commandments of God without fault', then go by yourself into a lonely place,³ recollect yourself, gather your thoughts together, and give your soul this good advice: 'Why are you cast down, my soul, and why do you trouble me? Hope in God, for I shall praise him still; for it is my God, not myself, who works my

1.62.¹ Phil 2:8.   1.64.² Mt. 13:25.
1.61.² Cf. *Ethical Discourse* 4; SCh 129:8f.   1.64.³ Mk 6:31.
1.64.¹ Mt 12:36.

salvation.[4] Who shall be justified by the works of the Law?[5] No living thing shall be reckoned just in your sight,[6] and yet, through my faith in God himself, I hope to be saved by the grace of his ineffable compassion. So get behind me Satan,[7] for I worship the Lord my God and him do I serve from my youth,[8] he who has the power to save me through his mercy alone. So get away from me! The God who made me in his own image and likeness shall make you powerless.[9]

1.65. God seeks nothing else from us men except that we do not sin; this alone. But this is not a work of law; it is rather a careful guarding of the image and dignity from above. In these things, affirmed in our nature and bearing the radiant garment of the Spirit, we shall abide in God and he in us.[1] We shall be called good, and sons of God by adoption, marked[2] in the light of our knowledge of God.

1.66. Listlessness and heaviness of body come on the soul though idleness and carelessness. They alienate the monk from his usual rule and give rise to discouragement and darkness in his thoughts. Then cowardly and blasphemous thoughts establish themselves in his heart, and he cannot go to his usual place of prayer because of this temptation by the demon of listlessness. So he gives in, and harbors bad feelings against the Maker of all things. But since you know the cause and origin of these things that come upon you, you must make every effort to go into your usual place of prayer and prostrate yourself before God, the lover of man.[1] Pray to him with sighs and tears in the affliction of your heart, |and ask him| to deliver you from the heaviness of listlessness and these wicked thoughts. If you strike hard and with perseverance, deliverance from these things will soon be given.

1.64.[4] Ps 42:6.   1.64.[7] Mk 8:10.   1.65.[1] 1 Jn 3:24.
1.64.[5] Gal 2:16   1.64.[8] Mt 4:10.   1.65.[2] Ps 4:7.
1.64.[6] Ps 143:2.   1.64.[9] Gen 1:26.
1.66.[1] See Clement of Alexandria, *Protreptikos* 10.67.20; PG 8:204.

1.67. If a man has achieved purity of heart, he has conquered cowardice. But if man is just on the point of achieving it, then sometimes he wins through, but at other times he is overcome. Yet when a man does not make any effort at all, he is completely oblivious to the fact that he is the friend of the passions and the demons. Such a man adds presumption to the sickness of pride, thinking he is something special when in fact he is nothing at all;[1] or rather he is the slave of cowardice, trembling like a nervous child and being afraid where, for those who fear the Lord, there is neither fear nor cowardice.[2]

1.68. When a man fears God he is no longer afraid of the assaults of demons or their feeble sttacks, or even of the threats of wicked men. He is wholly like a flame or a burning fire. Day and night he goes round in hidden and lonely places, banishing the demons. It is they who run away, not he, in case they are swallowed up in the burning rays of divine fire that radiate from him.

1.69. When a man walks in the fear of God he knows no fear, even if he were to be surrounded by wicked men. He has the fear of God within him and wears the invincible armor of faith.[1] This makes him strong and able to take on anything, even things which seem difficult or impossible to most people. Such a man is like a giant surrounded by monkeys, or a roaring lion among dogs and foxes. He goes forward trusting in the Lord and the constancy of his will to strike and paralyze his foes. He wields the blazing club of the word in wisdom.[2]

1.70. If you are dominated by cowardice, do not be surprised if you tremble with fear at everything. You are still weak and imperfect, like a child afraid of goblins. Cowardice

1.67.[1] Gal 6:3.
1.67.[2] Ps 14:5.
1.67.[3] Ps 27:1.

1.69.[1] Eph 6:11.
1.69.[2] Cf. 2 Cor 6:7.

is a childish fault which makes the proud soul look ridiculous. So do not try to bandy words or compose refutations against such a demon; words are no use when the soul is upset and trembling. Leave these things to one side, humble your reason as much as you can, and you will soon feel cowardice melt away.

1.71. A certain man was once seized by listlessness. His mind was dark and empty; his soul wandered. Little by little the fervor in his heart was stifled, the fire of the Spirit within him died down, and all the dwelling of his body became filled with smoke. At the same time a great weariness came over his limbs as a result of this apathy, and it made him feel drowsy all the time and forced him to abandon his usual routine. He resisted all this with vigils and fasting, but as soon as he had overcome his drowsiness, his heart hardened in self-conceit, and when fervor was driven out, cowardice slipped in. So as soon as he felt this within him, he left his cell at an unaccustomed hour and came away into the gloom of a dark place. There he stood lifting his hands to heaven. He marked himself with the sign of the cross and lifted the eyes of his soul to God. No sooner had he humbled his reason than the demon of cowardice began to leave him. Yet, even stronger than the last, the terrible enemy of pride crept into his reason and tried to seize and deliver it again to the demon of cowardice. When he realized this, he was amazed, and with fervor begged God to snatch his soul away from these snares of the devil.

1.72. It seems to me that few people understand the extent of the cunning wickedness of these demons and the way in which they assist one another. I have known the demon of cowardice to fight and work together with | that of | listlessness. One comes to the aid of the other and reinforces him. The first brings fear and obduracy into the soul; the second produces darkness, negligence, blindness of heart and mind,

and finally despair. Listlessness is a real trial for all those engaged in the spiritual struggle, but it becomes for them the
ambassador of humility.

1.73. Usually the demon of listlessness makes special as-
sault on those who are advanced in prayer or devoted to the
practice of prayer. No other demon can prevail against such
men. This could be part of the |divine| economy which
permits it some force against them, but I am more inclined to
think that it draws its force from the vagaries of our bodies.
What I am saying is this: when I have eaten well and my
stomach is full, and I have slept as long as I can, then passion
becomes lord of my mind and I am the worse for it. But if,
on the other hand, I mortify myself excessively, I make my
mind clouded and slow, and immediately fall into the same
passion. It is just like the atmospheric humidity[1] and the op-
pressive vapors of the southern wind, for these have the same
effect on ascetics.

1.74. Accidie is the death of mind and soul. If God allowed it to work its full power against us, no ascetic could
ever be saved. So while we should resist it according to our
ability, it is for God to awaken us mystically and clearly
give us the victory over it. It is impossible for dead men to
rise again without the help of the one who raised himself
from the dead.

1.75. Whenever the mind is carried away and sinks down
into self-conceit, whenever it imagines that it can do something on its own in this struggle, then the unseen grace which
illumines it is immediately taken away and it is soon left
empty. Straightaway it receives the proof of its own weakness, for the passions hurl themselves upon it like wild dogs
seeking to devour it. It is wholly at a loss and, having nowhere to run for safety, it takes refuge through humility in
the Lord who has the power to save it.

1.73.[1] *Krasis*, the composition of the air.

1.76. When a man has completely abandoned the world, it seems to him that he is living in a remote desert, full of wild beasts.[1] He is filled with unutterable fear and indescribable trembling, and cries to God like Jonah from the whale, from the sea of this life,[2] or like Daniel[3] from the pit of the lions and the fierce passions, or like the three children[4] from the burning furnace and the flames of innate desire, or like Manasseh[5] from the brazen statue of this earthly mortal body. The Lord hears him and delivers him from the abyss of ignorance and the love of this world, just like the prophet who came out of the whale, never to go back again. He delivers him, as he delivered Daniel, from the pit of desire and evil thoughts which rise up to devour the souls of men. Against the attacks of the fires of passion which consume and destroy the soul, pushing and pulling it into evil acts, he guards it from burning and sprinkles it with the dew of the Holy Spirit as he did with the three Israelites. |God| lifts him from this dull, earthly, and passible flesh and saves him from falling in humiliation in order to make him a son of light, of the day.[6] Even on this earth, he gives him a foretaste of immortality.

1.77. When a soul persists in remaining in the lowness of the body, seeking out its pleasures and holding on to the glory of men — or even if it does not do this to a great extent but nonetheless remains sensible to all the pleasurable effluences of this atmosphere — then it becomes absolutely inert and incapable of performing any virtue or divine command, just as if it were heavily burdened and weighed down by these evils I have mentioned. But when it is awakened by the trials of asceticism and tears of repentance, and has truly shaken off the burden of flesh; when it has washed away the

1.76.[1] Cf. Mk 1:13 and Ps 63:1.   1.76.[3] Dan 6:18.
1.76.[2] Jonah 2:1.   1.76.[4] Dan 3:24.
1.76.[5] Cf. 2 Ch 33:12, and also the apocryphal *Prayer of Manasseh*.
1.76.[6] 1 Thess 5:5, Jn 12:36, Eph 5:8.

salt-water of earthly preoccupations in floods of tears; when
it has transcended the meanness of visible reality and attained
to the pure light; and when it has been found worthy to be
freed from the tyranny of the passions, then it cries out to
God like the prophet: 'You have torn off my sackcloth and
girded me with gladness. And so my glory shall sing to you
and I shall not be confounded.'[1]

1.78. The divine Scriptures indicate that there are three
places where the mind likes to dwell.[1] I would say myself
that there are really two such places—not that I want to
teach the contrary to Scripture, God forbid, but I do not
count the middle position between the first and the last.
What I mean is that if a man travels from one city to the next
or from one region to another, he does not name his entire
passage after one town or region, especially if he has seen
many beautiful things along the way. When the [sacred
writer] left Egypt for the promised land and settled there,
he recalled everything that had happened during his travels
and recounted them to everybody. But he did not talk about
passing from a first to a second city or region, and then from
a second to a third. No, he spoke of passing from slavery to
freedom, from darkness into light, and from captivity to a
re-establishment in his own fatherland. This applies to our
human minds too, but here it is usually a case of passing from
passibility to impassibility, from the slavery of the passions
to the freedom of the Spirit, from unnatural obsessions
(which the spiritual law speaks of as a captivity[2]) to the
transcending of nature, from the stormy seas of life to a gen-

1.77.[1] Ps 30:11.
1.78.[1] A somewhat obscure text regarding the Scripture to which
he refers, though we may possibly discern *the carnal mind* (Rom.
8:7, Eph 2:3, Col 2:18), the *virtuous mind* that seeks God (Acts
20:19, Rom 7:25, 2 Tim 1:7), and the *spiritual mind* which is in union
with God (1 Cor 2:16). Such exegesis may lie behind Symeon's
thought here.
1.78.[2] Cf. Rom 7:5-6, 23.

tle calm beyond the world, from the bitterness of the cares and sorrows of this life to a joy that cannot be described and the banishment of all care, and from a multitude of desires that throng around and trouble us to one single desire: to possess and love God completely.

1.79. When the mind moves from visible realities to those that cannot be seen, no longer resting in sensible things but in those that transcend the senses, then this makes us oblivious[1] to all that we have left behind. This is what I mean by stillness,[2] and the home and resting-place of stillness. No one found worthy to enter here will ever come back down again as did Moses after spending forty days and nights on the mountain.[3] Such a man is certain that it is good to be there,[4] and he will never again return to the things below. From that time on, the Trinity dwells in him and he in the trinity. It is just as if he were in the kingdom of heaven, for love clearly rules him and keeps him from falling.

1.80. It is not only the hesychast or the simple monk[1] who should be free from cares and completely liberated from the pressing affairs of life; it applies to the *higoumenon*[2] too, and the superior of many men, and even someone with a ministry. For if we have worries we find ourselves disobeying the Lord's command: 'Do not be concerned about your lives, what you eat, what you drink, what you wear. The pagans search after all these things.'[3] And again: 'See that your hearts are never weighed down with gluttony and drunkenness and the worries of this life.'[4]

1.81. When a man's thoughts are filled with anxiety about

1.79.[1] *Lethe*: the mythical waters of oblivion separating the worlds.
1.79.[2] *Hesychia*.
1.79.[3] Cf. 2 Cor 3. The idea of transfiguration underlies Symeon's thought here.
1.79.[4] Cf. Lk 9:33.
1.80.[1] *Upostammenos*.   1.80.[3] Mt 6:25.
1.80.[2] Monastic superior.   1.80.[4] Lk 21:34.

the affairs of life, he is not free. He is oppressed and enslaved by these anxieties, and worries either about himself or about others. But a man who is free from these things worries about neither his own life nor that of others — even if he is a bishop, or *higoumenon*, or deacon. Nonetheless he does not forget or neglect anything at all, even the least and most insignificant details.[1] He pleases God in all that he does and all he achieves, so that in all things and in all his life he remains free from anxiety.

1.82. There can be useless worry and carefree action, and likewise, carefree work and anxious inactivity. This is what the Lord himself referred to in the saying: 'Even now my Father is working and I too work.'[1] And again: 'Do not work for food that cannot last, but for that which abides to eternal life.'[2] He does not abolish work, but teaches us to work without worrying. And when he says: 'What man for all his anxiety can add a single cubit to his height?'[3] he abolishes useless anxiety. But with regard to what can be useful, he says: 'Why do you worry about food or clothes? Do you not see the lilies of the field, how they grow in abundance, and the birds of the heavens, how they are fed?'[4] In this way the Lord condemns one way and praises the other, and he teaches us that we should make it our care to work without care, and that once we are free from anxiety we should avoid all activity that does not help us.

1.83. Do not destroy your own house in trying to build up your neighbor's. Reckon up how tiring and difficult the work will be.[1] Otherwise, once you start, you might pull down your own house and then find you have no strength to build your neighbor's.

1.84. As long as you still have not achieved perfect indifference to the affairs and the goods of life, have no desire to

1.81.[1] Mt 18:10.   1.82.[2] Jn 6:27.   1.82.[4] Mt 6:28.
1.82.[1] Jn 5:17.   1.82.[3] Mt 6:27.   1.83.[1] Lk 14:28-30.

takc the direction of these matters into your own hands, and
then you yourself will not be taken by them. [For if that
happens,] instead of receiving the reward of your steward-
ship, you will be charged with theft and sacrilege. If however your superior obliges you to do this, be as careful as a
man carrying a blazing flame. And as long as you check the
pretensions of your thoughts by confession and repentance,
you will be preserved by the prayer of your superior.

1.85. If a man has not achieved impassibility, he does not
know what impassibility is, and cannot believe that anyone
on earth could possess it. If he has not first renounced himself[1] and freely poured out his blood for this truly blessed
life, how could he understand that someone else has really
done all this to gain impassibility? It is the same with a man
who thinks he possesses the Holy Spirit but really does not.
When he hears about the energies of the Holy Spirit working
in those who truly possess him, he never believes that there is
someone in this generation who is equal to the apostles of
Christ and the saints of old,[2] who is inspired and moved by
the Spirit, and who sees him intuitively and perceptibly.[3]
For when a man judges the affairs of his fellows for good or
evil, he can do so only on the basis of his personal condition.

1.86. The impassibility of the soul is one thing; the impassibility of the body is another. The first can even sanctify
the body by its own brilliance and the radiance of the Spirit,
but that of the body alone cannot bring anything to the man
who has it.

1.87. The immobility of our spiritual and physical members is one thing, but the acquisition of virtues is another.
The first depends on nature, but the second governs all the
natural motions.

1.85.[1] Mt 16:24.
1.85.[2] Cf. *Chapters* 3:85-7.
1.85.[3] *Euaisthētōs kai gnōstōs*, as in *Chapters* 1:53.

1.88. To have no desire for the attractions and pleasures of the world is not the same thing as aspiring after the good things that are eternal and invisible. They are two distinct things. Many people despise the first, but few give thought to the second.

1.89. If it is one thing to shun the praises of men and not go looking for them, it is not the same as being attached to the glory of God. There is a great difference between them. Many men who are still ruled by their passions have rejected the first, but very few have been worthy of receiving the second, and then only through great pain and labor.

1.90. It is one thing to be content with shabby clothes and have no desire for magnificent array, but a different matter to put on the light of God. They are two different things. Caught up in a myriad desires, some have easily been negligent, but only they [put on the light] who constantly search for it through all kinds of penitence; those who become children of light and of the day through the fulfilment of the commandments.[1]

1.91. It is one thing to speak with humility, but another thing again to have a humble heart. Humility is one thing; the fruit and flower of humility are another. The beauty of this fruit and the good things it brings are quite distinct, and the energies which come from this fruit are different again. Of all these things that lead us to humility, some are within our power and some are not. We can conceptualize them, understand them, meditate on them, talk about them, and even put them into practice, but when it comes to that holy humility itself and all its consequent graces, characters, and powers, then this is all a gift of God. It is not from us. Yet no man would ever be counted worthy if he had not first taken care to sow the seeds of all that he was able to do himself.

1.90.[1] Cf. Eph 5:8, 1 Thess 5:5.

Holiness

1.92. ⌈You may not be annoyed by insults or injuries or by trials and afflictions, but it is quite a different matter to be able to think well of it all, and another matter again to pray for all those who do such things to you. You may even love them from your soul, but it is a different matter again to hold each one of their faces etched on your mind and to embrace them impassibly like true friends, with tears of sincere love and without a trace of revulsion to be found in your soul. But greater than all these things we have spoken of is the ability to remain in the same calm state, without flaring up, even in the time of trial itself, when men abuse you to your face, accuse you, hound and condemn you, despise and spit on you, even those who keep the appearances of friendship but do the same things behind your back, for they cannot hide it completely. And yet I am sure that there is something even greater still, and that is to cover all your sufferings with total oblivion, never to dwell on anything that has happened, whether your persecutors are near or far away, and to greet them at reunions and banquets as your friends, without a backward glance at the past.⌋

1.93. To remember God is not the same thing as to love God. To fear him is not the same as to keep his commandments. They are quite different things, though they become one in those who are perfect and impassible.

1.94. It is one thing to avoid sin but another matter to practise the commandments. The former is for those who have reached the first stage of impassibility; the latter for those who have struggled and lived in accordance with the Gospel.

1.95. Idleness is not the same thing as spiritual stillness,[1] and this stillness is not the same thing as silence. [All three] are quite distinct. The first pertains to those who have no desire to participate in the good things of God or even to

1.95[1] *Hesychia.*

succeed in good things; the second pertains to those who constantly make time for the knowledge of God, who are attentive to the words of innate wisdom, who search the depths of the Spirit and are initiated into the awesome mysteries of God;[2] the third pertains to those who commit themselves to intellectual pursuits and give close scrutiny to their thoughts.

hesychasm

1.96. It can hardly be called an exile when you just travel from one place to another. The two things are totally different. Those who struggle or are dragged along by idleness or instability of mind can be said to travel, and perhaps even those whose new fervor leads them into even greater efforts; but only those who are crucified to the world and the affairs of the world can be said to be in exile, men who long for one thing only, to be forevermore with the one God and his angels and never to return to the things of men.

1.97. To fight one's enemies and drive them back is not the same thing as defeating them once and for all, routing them, and putting them to death. The first pertains to those high-minded men who struggle, but the second is for those who are perfect and impassible.

1.98. All these things are the works of the saints who walk in the light of impassibility. But for men who realize that they are far from such things, let no one mislead them and may they never deceive their own souls. They know themselves that they walk vainly as if in the darkness.[1]

1.99. Many men have gone after these things for many different reasons, but few indeed have undertaken to practise them in the innate fear and love of God. Only these, as they are helped by grace from above, can quickly succeed in the

1.95.[2] Cf. Mt 13:11.
1.98.[1] Symeon urges the need for maturity in the spiritual life, and a discernment not incompatible with his insistence on the need for a 'spiritual father'.

practice of virtue and press on to the things we have spoken
of. The rest give up and wander about as if they were in that
desert of which it is said, 'and there is no pathway';[1] or again,
'I have abandoned them to the desires of their hearts and they
shall walk according to their desires'.[2]

1.100. Fervor is a most beautiful thing, and when it has
brought a man to the experience of these things he will know
the meaning of my words. Anyone else might grasp the
literal sense of the words, but will only be able to manage
theoretical ideas of the spiritual and intellectual implications.
In fact, he will build for himself deceptive fictions in his
thoughts, but he will be very far from these truths we have
spoken of, and riddled with deceits.

1.101. When you have overcome the baseness of the body
through many griefs and sorrows and have conquered all its
slaveries, you can carry it round with you as a light weight.
It is like a spiritual body, and is neither tired nor hungry nor
thirsty. When this is so, you will see him who is beyond all
understanding[1] more clearly than in any mirror. With your
eyes opened by tears, you will see him whom no man has ever
seen,[2] and then, your soul stung with desire for his love, you
will chant a lament mingled with tears. On that day remember me and pray for this poor man, for you will have achieved
union with God and a boldness before him which shall never
be confounded.

1.99.[1] Ps 107:40.   1.101.[1] 1 Cor 13:12.
1.99.[2] Ps 81:12.   1.101.[2] Jn 1:18.

OTHER THEOLOGICAL AND GNOSTIC CHAPTERS

(25)

2.1. PENITENCE IS NOT for the man who contem-) ?
plates,[1] just as contemplation is not for the man /
who must do penance. As far as [is] the rising
from the setting of the sun,[2] so does contemplation surpass
penitence. A man who repents and does penitential works
is like a sick and diseased person, or a wretched beggar cry-
ing out for alms, but the contemplative is someone who lives
in the courts of the emperor, who wears splendid and royal
garments. He is a confidant of the emperor, speaking with
him constantly, and hour by hour listening directly to his
commands and wishes.

2.2. As the knowledge of God develops within us, it becomes the cause and agent of our ignorance of all other beings, and this includes even God himself, for the immensity
of his brilliant light blinds us to everything. Sensation which
transcends all things is itself beyond sensation, and so it becomes insensible to everything outside itself. How can we
even call it a sensation when we cannot comprehend or grasp
these things at all? We do not know what they are like, or
their source and origin, or how they come about, let alone
what they are in themselves. Is it not true that these things
are really beyond sensation, and that the mind senses its own
weakness and finds itself insensible to something which is
beyond sensation? For that which the eye has not seen, or
ear heard, which has never entered into the heart of man,[1]
how shall it fall within the scope of sensation?

2.3. The Lord who has graced us with these super-sensible
things also gives us by his Spirit a new super-sensible sensa-

2.1.[1] *Theologein.*   2.1.[2] Ps 103:12.   2.2.[1] 1 Cor 2:9.

[63]

tion, so that through all our senses his gifts and graces, which supernaturally transcend sensation, can be sensed clearly and purely.

2.4. Any man who is insensible to the One[1] must be insensible to everything, just as he who senses the One thereby senses all things, even though he is outside all sensation. He stands within the sensation of all things, but is not overcome by this sensation.[2]

2.5. A man who is deaf to the word is deaf to all voices. But the man who hears the word can hear them all and still be deaf to everyone. He hears them all, but listens to none, except those who speak within the word. Even from these he takes nothing, for he listens only to the word who speaks silently through them.

2.6. When a man hears and sees and feels in this way, he will know the meaning of my words. It is obvious that a man who is incapable of understanding has not kept the senses of his soul alive and healthy, and so he still has not learned that he was made to look upon visible creation and to be initiated into the intelligible world. If he receives this honor, but then lowers himself to the level of the senseless beasts weighed down with burdens,[1] then he will stay like them and cannot be converted or called back or restored to his former dignity in accordance with the gift of the dispensation of our Lord and master Jesus Christ, the Son of God.[2]

2.7. While you are below do not search out the things above. Before you are lifted above do not have much to do with the things below. Then you will not fall and lose both, or rather be left with only the lower things.

2.8. When a man has been raised by the emperor from the direst poverty and given riches; when he has been clothed by

2.4.[1] Cf. *Chapters* 1:51.

2.4.[2] *Chapters* 2.4-6 parallel the *Catecheses* 28 (SCh 113:159-65) and *Chapters* 1:51-4.

2.6.[1] Ps 49:12.   2.6.[2] Eph 3:2, 7.

him in illustrious dignity and splendid garments, and even called to stand in his presence, then surely he regards his emperor with affection and loves him greatly as his benefactor? He takes note of the uniform he now bears and appreciates the dignity and the riches that have fallen to him. All this applies [in a similar way] to the monk who has truly abandoned the world and all its affairs, and come near to Christ. He has felt his call and has risen to the heights of spiritual contemplation by keeping the commandments. This man sees God himself without any error, and he clearly perceives the change that has come over him. He sees the grace of the Spirit always shining round him. This is called 'the garment' or 'the royal purple', but it is really Christ himself, if only those who believe are truly clothed in him.[1]

2.9. When a man is enriched with heavenly treasure—and I mean the presence and the indwelling of him who said: 'I and the Father shall come and make our home in him',[1]—then such a man knows in his very soul what immense grace he has received and what great happiness he contains within the palace of his heart. He speaks to God like one friend to another,[2] and in all boldness stands before the face of him who dwells in light inaccessible.[3]

2.10. Blessed is the man who believes these things. Thrice blessed is he who strives by means of good works and holy asceticism to understand these things I have spoken of. When a man has arrived at the heights of this condition through knowledge and contemplation, he is an angel. Indeed I could go further, for he has come to stand in the presence of God like a son of God.

2.11. When a man stands on the seashore he can see the endless waves of the ocean, but he can appreciate only a fraction of their whole extent. It is the same when a man has

2.8.[1] Gal 3:27.   2.9.[1] Jn 14:23.   2.9.[2] Ex 33:11.

2.9.[3] This concept continues the theme of theophany; see 1 Tim 6:16.

been counted worthy to gaze through contemplation on the boundless seas of the glory of God and to perceive him with his mind. He does not then see him as great as he is, but sees him only as great as is possible for the inner eyes of the soul that sees him.

2.12. It is like a man standing by the sea. If he is not content just to look, he can go into the waters as deeply as he wants. And if spiritual persons want it, they too can enter into participation with the light of God by means of contemplation, to the extent that they are inspired by desire and knowledge.

2.13. You can stand on the floodwalls and as long as you are not in the water you can see everything and grasp that whole ocean of water at a glance. But once you start to enter the water and become immersed, then the more you go down into it the more you lose sight of everything outside. It is the same for men who have come to participate in the divine light: the more they progress in divine knowledge, the more they fall into ignorance.[1]

2.14. When a man goes up to his knees or even to his waist in the water, he can still see everything outside the water quite clearly, but when he goes down to the bottom and is completely underwater he can see nothing of the things outside. He knows but one thing: that he is totally in the depths of the sea. It is exactly the same for men who make progress along the spiritual path and rise to the perfection of knowledge and contemplation.

2.15. When it happens that men who are advancing towards spiritual perfection are partly illuminated (that is, only their mind is enlightened), then they see the glory of the Lord intelligibly as if in a mirror. This grace from above teaches them knowledge[1] in a mystical way and confers a revelation of mysteries which leads them from the contem-

---

2.13.[1] A reprise of *Chapters* 1:51.   2.15.[1] Cf. *Chapters* 1:4.

plation of beings to the knowledge of him who is beyond all beings.

2.16. When men come close to perfection and yet see it only in part, they are frightened when they realize that it is impossible to grasp or seize what they see. As they penetrate into the light of knowledge, so do they receive an understanding of their own ignorance. When that which appeared to them rather indistinctly at first, showing itself as if in a mirror[1] and partly illuminating what their minds have grasped, sees fit to allow itself to be seen fully and to be united by participation with the man it has illumined, then it gathers him completely into itself. He is then totally within the depths of the Spirit, just as if he had been dropped into a bottomless abyss of illuminated waters. When this happens he rises ineffably into perfect unknowing, for he has transcended all knowledge.

2.17. When the mind is simple, or rather stripped of all conceptions and completely clothed in the simple light of God and hidden within it, it can find no other object in which it is established to which it can direct the motion of its thought. It remains in the depths of God's light and can see nothing outside. This is what the saying means: 'God is light.'[1] He is the supreme light, and for all those who have achieved it, the repose of all contemplation.

2.18. So although the mind is always in motion, it becomes motionless and empty of thought when it is completely covered by the divine darkness and light; or rather, it is in the vision, the sensation, and the enjoyment of these good things that it is established, for the depths of the waters of the sea are not exactly the same as the depths of the Holy Spirit, who is the living water of eternal life.[1] Everything to do with such [a life] is incomprehensible, beyond explanation or understanding, and once the mind has gone beyond visible and

2.16.[1] 1 Cor 13:12.   2.17.[1] 1 Jn 1:5.   2.18.[1] Jn 4:10.

conceptual reality, it moves and turns motionlessly round these things alone. It lives a life beyond life. It is light within light, though not a light to itself; for then it is not itself that it sees, but him who is above it; and the glory from him takes the mind away from its own thought so that it no longer knows itself.

2.19. A man who has achieved the measures of perfection is dead and not dead, for he lives in union with God because he no longer lives for himself.[1] He is a blind man, for he no longer sees by nature. He has transcended all natural vision because he has received new and better eyes, beyond comparison with those of nature, and so he sees beyond nature. He neither stirs nor moves, for all [need of] movement has been fulfilled in him. He is devoid of thoughts because he has become one with him who is beyond understanding. He rests where there is no more stirring of the mind, no movement at all, either of reflecting, reasoning, or understanding, for there is no way it can conceive or define something beyond thought or conception, and it is therefore in a state of rest. This rest is the stillness of blessedness beyond all sensation, through a true sensation of these indescribable delights which we truly enjoy without effort.

2.20. If someone has not been judged worthy to come to such a degree of perfection and gain possession of these good things, he can only blame himself. He must not excuse himself by saying that the whole thing is impossible, or that even if perfection does come, it comes on us unawares. No, he must know for certain from the scriptures that this is all possible and true, something that comes to effect and motivates our consciousness. A man only deprives himself of these good things as he is negligent, and when he breaks the commandments.[1]

2.19.[1] Rom 14:7.
2.20.[1] Cf. *Ethical Discourse* 10; SCh 129:274-6.

2.21. Many read the divine Scriptures and others hear them read. Few, however, are able to understand rightly the meaning and significance of what is read. They say that what the Scriptures speak of is impossible, or they judge them completely unworthy of faith, or interpret them wickedly. They reckon that things said of the present apply to the future, and they take the sayings about things to come as if they had already happened or were daily events. There is no right judgement among them,[1] and no true discernment in the affairs of God and man.

2.22. From the beginning God created two worlds, the visible and the invisible. But there is one single emperor of all visible reality, bearing in himself the characters of both worlds — what can be seen in him, that is, and what can only be comprehended about him. And in accordance with these two worlds there are two suns shining: one can be sensed, the other comprehended. What our sun is for this visible and sensory world, God is for the invisible and intelligible world. He is called the sun of righteousness and so he is.[1] So, then, we have these two suns, one sensible and one intelligible, just as there are two worlds, as I have said. One of these — that is the sensible world and all it constains — is illuminated by this sensible and visible sun, but the other — that is the intelligible world and all those in it — is illumined and enlightened by the sun of righteousness. So on the one hand, sensory things are illuminated by the sensible sun and, on the other, intelligible reality is illumined by the intelligible sun. But there is no full union or understanding or communion between the two, either from the intelligible to the sensible, or from the sensible world to the intelligible.[2]

2.23. Unique among all visible and intelligible things, man has been made two-fold by God. He has a body formed of the four elements with sensibility and breath and by these he

2.21.[1] Prov 28:5, 2 Tim 3:8.
2.22.[1] Mal 4:2.   2.22.[2] Cf. Lk 16:26.

communicates with the elements and lives within them. He also has a soul [endowed] with an immaterial, incorporeal rationality which is united with them in an inexpressible and indetectable way, and blended [with them] without mixture or confusion. This is what constitutes an individual man, an animal who is mortal and immortal, visible yet invisible, sensible and intelligible, and capable of seeing visible creation as well as of comprehending the intelligible. And just as the two suns each reserve their energies for their own worlds, so it follows that in the one human nature the first illumines the body and the other the soul. But each of the suns communicates its own light to the one it illumines by participation, either abundantly or poorly, depending on our receptivity.

2.24. The sensible sun is seen but does not see. The intelligible sun is seen by all those who are worthy, and also sees all men, but especially those who see it. The sensible sun neither speaks nor bestows the power of speech on others. The intelligible sun speaks with its friends and graces them all with speech. The sensible sun shines on our gardens, but merely evaporates the moisture from the soil by the heat of its rays; It is not this which feeds the plants and the seeds. But the intelligible [sun] reveals itself to the soul and does both things: it evaporates the moisture of the passions and cleans their corruption from them, and then it brings fertility to the land of the soul¹ where little by little the plants of the virtues are fostered and watered.

2.25. The sensible sun rises to shine on the world of sense and all it contains: men, wild beasts, flocks, or any other creature. On all of these it sheds its light equally, but then it goes down and again leaves in darkness the place where once it shone. The intelligible [sun] shines eternally, and was shining, complete in all complete reality, yet not con-

2.24.¹ A reference to the mystical and iconographic theme of the enclosed garden; see Sg 4:12.

tained by it. It is separate and distinct from its creatures, yet not separated from them. It is complete in all places, yet nowhere, and complete in all visible creatures yet completely outside them. It is complete in the visible and complete in the invisible. It is completely present everywhere, yet never completely in any place.

3.1. CHRIST IS THE BEGINNING,[1] the middle, and the end. He who is in the first[2] is in all, and as he is in the first so he is in the middle and the last as well. There is no difference between these things for him, just as there is neither barbarian, Scythian, Greek, nor Jew — only Christ who is in all and is all.[3]

3.2. From the first to the last, from head to foot, the holy Trinity reaches all men. It gathers them, joins and unites and binds them to itself, and by gathering them it makes them strong and impregnable. It reveals itself to each and every one, and makes itself known as one and the same. Such is God, in whom the last become first and the first last.[1]

3.3. We faithful ought to look upon all the faithful as one single being. We should consider that Christ is in each one. We should therefore be ready to give our life[1] willingly for the sake of our love for him. We have no right at all to say, or even to think, that a person is evil. As I have said, we should consider all of them good, and even if you see someone swept away by the passions, do not hate your brother; |hate instead| the passions which torment him. If he is tyrannized by desire and prejudice, you should groan all the more in case you yourself should be tempted,[2] for you are just as liable to the vicissitudes of unstable matter.

3.4. The intelligible orders of the higher powers are illumined by God from the first order to the second, and from

3.1.[1] 1 Cor 15:13.   3.2.[1] Mt 20:16.
3.1.[2] Col 1:18.   3.3.[1] Cf. Jn 15:13.
3.1.[3] Col 3:11.   3.3.[2] Gal 6:1.

there to all the others in the same way until the divine light passes through them all. The saints, too, are illumined in the same way by the divine angels, and as they are bound up and joined together in the bond of the Spirit,[1] they become their equals in honor and emulate them. These saints themselves come after the saints who preceded them, and from generation to generation[2] they join |their predecessors| through the practice of God's commandments. Like them, they are enlightened and receive this grace of God by participation. They become just like a golden chain with each one of them a link, bound to all the preceding saints in faith, love, and good works. So it is that they become one single chain in the one God, a chain that cannot easily be broken.[3]

3.5. But if a man is a false hypocrite or blameworthy in his conduct, if he is easily broken by a passion, or deficient through negligence in some matter, then he is not counted in the full company of these others. Instead, he is rejected as useless and unworthy in case he should cause the chain-link to break in times of stress, and bring about a division of what cannot be divided. This would cause distress to both parts, for both those who have gone before and those who come after would suffer equally from a separation.

3.6. If a man does not strive after union with the latest of all the saints,[1] in love and fervent longing, by means of humility, but rather bears a degree of unfaithfulness towards him, then he will never be wholly united or bound up with the earlier saints who preceded him, even if he thought he had perfect faith and perfect love[2] in the sight of God and all the saints. They shall cast him far from them since he would not accept with humility the place that was destined for him, which God set out for him before all ages.

3.4.[1] Cf. Eph 4:3.   3.4.[2] Is 9:27.
3.4.[3] See *Ethical Discourse* 1:6; SCh 122:227.
3.6.[1] Eph 3:8.   3.6.[2] Cf. 1 Cor 13:2.

3.7. Our sorrow before God is preceded by humility and followed by joy and a happiness that cannot be expressed. And this humility before God gives birth to the hope of salvation. The more a person thinks in his soul that he is the most sinful of men, the more does hope increase and flourish within his heart by this humility, giving us the confidence that it will be our salvation.

3.8. When a man penetrates the depths of humility and recognizes that he is unworthy to be saved, his sorrow releases springs of tears, and as a consequence spiritual joy floods out in his heart. In this way, hope rises out of this spring, grows with it, and strengthens our certainty of being saved.

3.9. Each man must look at himself and understand himself. He must not rely only on this hope to the exclusion of spiritual humility and sorrow before God, nor on humility and tears without the spiritual joy and hope that must accompany them.

3.10. There is a false kind of humility which rises from careless neglect or the pangs of conscience. People who have this think it ushers in salvation, but it does not, for it does not have as its companion that sorrow which alone is the bringer of joy.

3.11. There is a sorrow that has no spiritual humility about it, and people who feel this think it washes away their sins. They are, however, foolishly mistaken, for they do not have the sweetness of the Spirit which comes mystically in the inner treasury of the soul, and they do not taste the goodness of the Lord.[1] Such people are quickly roused to anger and cannot renounce the world and worldly things. Yet when a man does not renounce all these things completely and hate them from his very soul, there is no way he can hold on to any firm or assured hope of salvation. He will always be buf-

3.11.[1] Ps 34:8.

feted by doubts because he did not build his house upon the rock.[2]

3.12. Sorrow works in two ways: it is like water because it quenches all the fire of passion with tears and washes the soul clean of stains, and it is like a fire which gives life by the presence of the Holy Spirit. It kindles, blazes up, and warms the heart, and inflames it with love and desire for God.

3.13. You must see and understand these energies that come to you through humility and sorrow, and you should weigh up at the proper time the benefits they have brought you. For those who are just beginning this means the overthrow of all earthly care, the renunciation of all one's family and friends with detachment, and a care-free disdain for all wealth and business, not just to the last needle, but even down to one's own body.

3.14. If you throw dust over the flames of a blazing furnace, you put it out, and in the same way, all the cares of life[1] and all one's shabby attachments, even the most trivial, utterly annihilate the fervor that was alight in your heart at the beginning.

3.15. When a man has joyfully come to the renunciation of all external activities, people, and affairs, in a considered maturity of heart, and has arrived at such an oblivion of them that it seems as if he has scaled the walls of attachment, then such a man becomes an alien to the world and all it contains. He concentrates his mind and gives his attention only to remembering and thinking about his death. From then on he thinks constantly about judgement and retribution. Such thoughts and meditations on these things hold him prisoner and fill him with unspeakable dread.

3.16. When a man carries this fear of judgement deep within, he is like a condemned man loaded with chains upon the stage of this life. He is dragged along by fear as if it were

3.11.[2] Lk 6:48.   3.14.[1] Lk 21:34.

his executioner, and it seems as if he goes off to death thinking only of the grief and suffering he will have to undergo in the everlasting punishment. Since all this is borne indelibly in his heart, he is afraid, and can have no time for the affairs of men. He always behaves as if he were already affixed to the cross and suffering the terrible pains of death. He no longer allows himself to look anyone in the eyes, and no longer cares about the honor or dishonor of men. In his heart he reckons that he is worthy of all dishonor and shame, so he no longer cares about the injuries that may befall him.

3.17. When a man fosters the fear of death in his heart, all food and drink and fine clothes disgust him. He gets no pleasure from eating his bread or drinking water, and merely supplies the needs of his body in order to keep it alive. Such a man has renounced all self-will and has become the slave of all, at the beck and call of all who command him.

3.18. When the fear of retribution leads a man to subject himself as a slave to his fathers under God, he will not choose anything that alleviates the grief of his heart or slackens the chain of fear, even if he is ordered to do so. Nor will he listen when men advise these things, either through friendship, flattery, or by way of dominance. Instead, he will hold in greater esteem everything that increases his grief and will long for anything that will bind his chains tighter. He will love whatever strengthens his executioners and will remain here as if he never expected to be freed. The hope of release lightens one's grief and is unprofitable for those who have fervently repented.

3.19. The fear of retribution and the grief this produces are most useful for anyone who starts to live a life pleasing to God. If anyone thinks he can make a start without such grief or without this chain and executioner, he has not only founded his efforts on the sand,[1] but has even thought he

3.19.[1] Mt 7:26.

could build his house in mid-air without any foundations at all. It is altogether impossible. Yet this grief gives birth to almost every joy; this chain breaks the chains of all sin and passions; and this executioner deals out not death but everlasting life.

3.20. When a man does not try to escape or avoid this grief which is born of the fear of eternal retribution, but follows after it with ready heart and wraps his chains around him all the more, he will then progress more rapidly until he comes to stand before the face of the King of Kings. On that day, when he perceives his glory no matter how obscurely, his chains shall immediately fall away. The executioner (who is fear) will run far away from him, and the grief in his heart will be turned into joy.[1] He will feel this sensibly as a spring gushing out, an endless river of tears, and he will understand it intelligibly as peace, sweetness, and unspeakable tenderness. It is also a source of manly strength and freedom | which enables us to | run without hindrance in complete obedience to the commandments of God.[2] Until now, beginners had found this impossible; it was a privilege reserved for those who were already in the midst of their ascent. But for those who are perfected this spring becomes a light for their hearts so suddenly converted and transformed.

3.21. When a man has within him the light of the all-holy Spirit, he cannot bear the sight and so he falls prostrate on the ground. He cries out and shouts, driven out of his senses by immense fear. He is like someone who sees or feels something beyond nature, reason, and understanding. It is as if his entrails were touched by fire and scorched with flames. He cannot bear this burning[1] and becomes like someone outside himself, and because he does not have the strength | to endure |, he pours out an endless flood of tears which refreshes him and rouses up the flame of his desire. His tears become

3.20.[1] Jn 16:20.   3.20.[2] Ps 119:32.   3.21.[1] Cf. Jer 20:9.

more abundant and, when he is purified in their flood, he shines with a greater brilliance. Then, entirely on fire, he becomes like light and fulfills the saying: 'God is made one with the gods and becomes known.'² This occurs insofar as he is already united to those who are attached to him, and revealed to those who know him.

3.22. To the extent that God wants to be known by us, he reveals himself. And as much as he is revealed, so is he seen and known by those who are worthy. But no one can ever experience or see this if he is not first united to the all-holy Spirit, or if he has not acquired a humble, pure, simple, and contrite heart¹ through much effort and toil.

3.23. Let no one deceive us with empty words¹ or lead us astray before |we have experienced| sorrow and tears, for |without these| there is no repentance or true conversion or fear of God in our hearts. We must never have accused ourselves, and our soul must not have thought about future judgement and eternal punishments. If it had acquired or gone into these things, tears would have flooded out immediately. Without them our withered hearts could never be softened and our souls could never achieve spiritual humility or be strong enough to be humble. But if a man is not like this, he cannot be united with the Holy Spirit, and if he is not united with him through purification, he cannot come to the knowledge and contemplation of God or be worthy to be taught about the mystical virtues of humility.

3.24. If you tried to expound rhetoric or philosophy to someone who had just learned to pronounce the alphabet, it would be worse than useless. It would put him off and make him neglectful of those things he had begun to learn, because his intelligence would not be able to grasp anything of what you said. And it is the same if you should speak about per-

---

3.21.² The saying is unidentified, perhaps a patristic gloss on Gen 3:22.

3.22.¹ Ps 51:17.   3.23.¹ Eph 5:6.

fection to those who are just beginning, especially the lazier
ones. It would not only be useless in itself, but would also
make them regress still further. They would peer up at the
summit of excellence and, having weighed up how distant
they are from the top, would decide that it was impossible for
them to reach it. They would therefore despise the things
they have already achieved as useless, and sink into despair.

3.25. When men who are dominated and ruled by passions
hear about someone who is perfect before God—that he considers himself more unclean than any man, animal, or beast,
that he rejoices when he is dishonored and returns blessings
when he is injured, that he endures all persecutions and even
prays for his enemies[1] with tears and grief in his heart, calling
on God and interceding on their behalf—then they do not
believe at first that their own efforts could make them like
this. Then, when they are proved wrong by the divine
Scriptures and contradicted by the saints who truly witness
these qualities, they say that they are not strong enough to
attain such things. And finally, when they hear that they
cannot be saved until they achieve this, they despair of themselves because they are unwilling to make a final break with
evil and repent of their sins.

3.26.[1] There are some who pretend to be virtuous and appear in sheep's clothing as something else;[2] but in the inner
man[3] they are totally different, perhaps brimming over with
every kind of unrighteousness or filled up with jealousy, intrigue, and stinking pleasures. The masses honor such people
as saints who have transcended the passions, but since the
eye of their soul is not clear they cannot recognize such men
by their fruits.[4] And yet, when men keep their hearts in
piety, virtue, and simplicity, and really are saintly, then they

3.25.[1] Cf. Mt 5:11-2, 44.
3.26.[1] For *Chapters* 26-8, see *Ethical Discourse* 1.6, 1.36; SCh 122:
227.
3.26.[2] Mt 7:15-6.   3.26.[3] Rom 7:22.   3.26.[4] Mt 7:16.

misjudge them as being like the rest of men, and they are scorned and passed over.

3.27. They look upon a showy talker as a spiritual master, but when a man is silent and careful of his words, they think he must be an inarticulate yokel.

3.28. Those who are haughty and sick with the devil's pride cast away anyone who cries out in the Holy Spirit as if he were himself a haughty and proud man. This is because his words hit them, but do not strike home. But when a man gives them well-turned phrases[1] from himself or from what he has learned, and lies to them about their salvation, then they praise him boundlessly and gladly accept him. None of these people, then, is truly capable of seeing the facts or judging objectively.

3.29. God says: 'Blessed are the pure in heart for they shall see God.'[1] There is no one virtue, then, or even two or ten, which can bring about a pure heart. It is a matter for all of them together, joined as if they were one single entity and striving after the final goal. But even then they cannot produce a pure heart by themselves without the presence and the actions of the Spirit. The smith can use his tools with all his skill, but he cannot produce anything at all without the action of the fire, and in just the same way a man can do all things using the tools of the virtues, but they will not clean away dirt and corruption from the soul. Without the presence of the fire of the Spirit they will be feeble and useless.

3.30. Where there is profound humility you will find abundant tears, and where you have these you will find the presence of the holy and adorable Spirit. When this [presence] arrives, all purity and holiness come to the man it inspires. Then God appears to him and God looks on him. It is

3.28.[1] *Tornologounta*, see *Life*, p. 65, where Nicetas draws our attention to a similar phrase in Symeon's *Letter to Stephen of Nicomedia*, v. 61: *tois lalousi torneutōs kai plousiōs*.

3.29.[1] Mt 5:8.

said: 'On whom shall I look except the man of gentle stillness who trembles at my words?'[1]

3.31 Man can fight against the passions but not root them out altogether. He has received the power to refuse to do evil, but not to be free from [evil] thoughts. Yet piety is not just a matter of doing what is good, it also means not even thinking anything that is evil. So the man who has evil thoughts is unable to achieve a pure heart. How could he, when these things have smudged him like dirt on a mirror?

3.32. It seems to me that having a pure heart is not simply a matter of not being swept away by passion; it also involves avoiding any inclination of mind to whatever is evil or profane, and having within oneself one thing alone: recollection of God in irrepressible love. When nothing external interrupts our contemplation, our eye can see God purely in pure light.

3.33. I will say this: being impassible is more than a matter of not expressing the passions; it also involves abandoning all desire for them and even purging our mind of any thought about them. Then, if we so desire, we can rise above the heavens and go outside all visible and sensible reality. It is as if our senses had closed down and our mind had penetrated things beyond sensation, carrying the senses with it by its force like an eagle [lifting] its wings.

3.34. The mind cannot manifest its own activities without the senses, and without the mind there is no way the senses can show theirs.

3.35. The heart is said to be pure, and really is pure, when it finds no profane thought or fantasy within it. It is then consecrated and united with God to such an extent that it no longer remembers either the joys or the sorrows of this life. It rises on contemplation as if into the third heaven,[1] and is snatched up to paradise to look upon the pledges of the good

3.30.[1] Is 62:2.   3.35.[1] 2 Cor 12:2-4.

things promised to the saints. Even on earth it is a witness to these eternal goods in so far as human nature is capable [of comprehending them]. This is truly the sign and the sure indication of the pure heart by which a man can know the measure of his purity and see himself as if in a mirror.

3.36.[1] When a person is outside the house he cannot see those who are shut up inside, and in the same way the man who is crucified—that is, dead to the world—has no sensation of the things of the world.

3.37. A dead body does not have the slightest sensation either of living things or of the other corpses lying beside it, and it is just the same with the man who is outside the world in the Spirit and lives with God. He too is unable to have any sensation of the world or feeling for its affairs, even though he is still subject to bodily necessities.

3.38. [There is a death before death and a resurrection of souls before the resurrection of the bodies.] It is a fact, a power, an experience, a truth. When mortal wisdom fades away before the immortal mind and death is driven off by life, then it is as if the soul rises from the dead. It sees and recognizes itself just like someone waking from his sleep. It recognizes the God who raised it up, and as it gazes on him and renders thanks, it rises above the senses and the whole world. It is then filled with ineffable pleasure and all the stirrings of its thought lie down to rest in him.

3.39. There are the things which we contribute and there are the things given us from on high by God. To the extent that we are purified through holy toils and labors, we are illumined by the light, so are we purified in tears. On the one hand we bring out our own resources, and on the other we receive the gift from on high.

3.40. There are many who have made their contribution without receiving that which God usually gives. You can see

3.36.[1] *Chapters 36-8 parallel Ethical Discourse* 1.6; SCh 122:227.

this in the conduct and treatment of Cain and Esau.[1] This is because if anyone makes his offering without a right mind and pious intention and fervent faith, or without great humility, then God will not look upon him and will not receive his offerings. If someone makes an offering without these things then He will not respond.

3.41. The world and worldly persons are dead in regard to the saints. So even when they look, they do not see their good works, and when they listen they cannot grasp[1] the divine words they speak in the Holy Spirit. But spiritual persons cannot see the evil deeds of wicked and profane men, or understand their words of passion. In their turn they look upon the things of the world, but do not see and listen to the traffic of the world as if they did not hear. There is, then, no communion between them and the others, or between these and the spiritual ones.

3.42. The difference between light and darkness is obvious and no confusion is possible, for as he says: 'What is there in common between light and darkness or between the believer and the unbeliever?'[1] There is just as great a difference and separation between those who have the Holy Spirit and those who do not. The first have their citizenship in heaven,[2] and from being men have already become angels. But the others are still in the darkness of their fathers, sitting in the shadow of death,[3] pinned to the earth and its concerns. The former are lit up by the unfading, unintelligible light, and see both themselves and their fellows, but the others have only the sensible light. Although they see themselves and their fellows dying each day, still they do not understand that they are men and that they die like men.[4] Since they do not know, they do not believe, either about the judgement or that there will be a resurrection and a retribution to each man according to his conduct.

3.40.[1] Gen 4.　　　3.42.[1] 2 Cor 6:15.　　3.42.[3] Cf. Ps 107:10.
3.41.[1] Cf. Mt. 13:13.　3.42.[2] Phil 3:20.　　3.42.[4] Ps 82:7.

3.43. If the Holy Spirit is with you, the energies he works in you will make you understand perfectly what the apostle was talking about when he said: 'Where the Spirit of the Lord is, there is freedom,'¹ and again: 'Though the body is dead through sinfulness, the spirit lives through righteousness,'² and again: 'Those who are of Christ have crucified the flesh with its passions and desires.'³ All who have been baptized in the Holy Spirit⁴ have put on the whole Christ.⁵ They are sons of the light,⁶ and walk in the light that does not fade.⁷ Although they look at the world, they do not see it, and though they listen to the noise of the world they do not hear.⁸ It is written of carnal men that seeing, they do not see, and hearing about divine affairs, they do not understand,⁹ nor are they able to grasp the things of the Spirit because to them they are foolishness.¹⁰ But I think this applies in the same way to those who have the Holy Spirit within them. They bear a body, but they are not in the flesh, for |Scripture| says: 'If the Spirit of God dwells in you, you are not in the flesh, but in the Spirit.'¹¹ These men are dead to the world and the world to them. 'The world is crucified to me,' it says, 'and I to the world.'¹²

3.44. When a man knows that these signs and wonders are taking place within him, he is truly a god-bearer, a vessel of wonder. He has God indwelling, the all-holy Spirit himself who speaks and works in him all the things that Paul spoke about. But the man who has not yet recognized these things in his heart must make no mistake: he is still flesh and blood, enveloped by the gloom of carnal desires. Flesh and blood, however, have no inheritance in the kingdom of God, for this is the Holy Spirit.¹

3.43.¹ 2 Cor 3:17. 3.43.⁶ Lk 6:8. 3.43.¹¹ Rom 8:9.
3.43.² Rom 8:10. 3.43.⁷ Cf. 1 Jn 1:7. 3.43.¹² Gal 6:14.
3.43.³ Gal 5:24. 3.43.⁸ Mt. 13:13.
3.43.⁴ Jn 1:33. 3.43.⁹ Lk 8:10. 3.44.¹ 1 Cor 15:50.
3.43.⁵ Gal 3:27. 3.43.¹⁰ 1 Cor 2:14.

3.45.[1] [We receive the remission of our sins at our divine baptism and we are freed from the ancient curse and sanctified by the presence of the Holy Spirit. But this is not yet that perfect grace of which the Scripture speaks: 'I shall dwell in them and walk therein.'[2] This applies only to those who are strong in faith and show it in their works, for if we fall back into evil and shameful deeds after our baptism, we completely throw away this very sanctification. It is in proportion to our repentance, confession, and tears that we receive the remission of our former sins, and as a consequence of this, sanctification and grace from on high.]

3.46. After repentance comes purification from the stain of shameful deeds, but after this comes participation in the Holy Spirit. Yet it is not an automatic thing; it depends on the faith, the disposition, and the humility of those who repent with their whole soul. Nor is this alone sufficient: we must also receive the complete remission of our sins from our father and sponsor.[1] This is why it is a good thing to repent each day as the commandment instructs us: 'Repent, for the kingdom of heaven draws near.'[2] This imposes upon us a duty without limit.

3.47. The grace of the all-holy Spirit is given as a pledge[1] to souls betrothed to Christ. When a young girl has no pledge, she has no guarantee that her marriage to her fiancé will really take place, and it is just the same for the soul if it does not receive the pledge of his grace or does not possess him intuitively within itself. It will then have no firm guarantee that it will be eternally united with its master and God, or that it will be mystically and ineffably joined to him, or that it will enjoy his inaccessible beauty.

baptism ?

3.45.[1] Cf. *Chapters* 1.36.   3.45.[2] 2 Cor 6:16.
3.46.[1] I.e. the spiritual father who stands over the monk's admission to the second baptism as the original sponsor did in the first.
3.46.[2] Mt 3:2.   3.47.[1] 2 Cor 1:12, Eph 1:14.

3.48. If the parchment of a contract does not bear the sig-
natures of reliable witnesses, the pledge is not a sure one. In
the same way, the illumination of grace is by no means assured until the commandments have been fulfilled and the
virtues acquired. ⌈As witnesses are to contracts, so is the
practice of the commandments and the virtues for this spiritual pledge.⌋ It is in this way that all who are going to be
saved[1] receive the full possession of the pledge.

works virtues joined to baptism

3.49. It is just as if the contract is first of all written down
through the practice of the commandments, then signed and
sealed by the virtues. It is then that Christ the bridegroom
gives the ring, or the pledge of the Spirit, to the soul, his bride.

3.50. Before the wedding, all that the bride receives from
her fiancé is a pledge. She waits until after the marriage to
receive the agreed dowry and the gifts promised in it. In the
same way, the bride, who is the Church of the faithful and
the soul of each one of us, at first receives only the pledge of
the spirit from Christ the bridegroom. She has to wait until
she leaves this earth to receive the everlasting gifts and the
kingdom of heaven. Yet the pledge gives her the complete
assurance that these agreements will not be deceptive.

3.51. Suppose the bridegroom were delayed on a journey[1]
or held back by some other business, and postponed the marriage for a while. If the bride is angered into scorning his love
and rips up or cancels the parchment which |contains| the
pledge, then she immediately loses all that she could hope for
from her fiancé. This applies to the soul in just the same way.
If a man who was struggling along should say: 'How long
am I to suffer?', and then completely neglect the hardships of
ascesis or become careless of the commandments and abandon his constant repentance, it is just as if he were to rip up
or cancel the contract. He immediately and irrevocably
loses the pledge, and with it, all that he could hope for from
God.

3.48.[1] Cf. Acts 2:47.   3.51.[1] Mt 25:5.

3.52. If a fiancée gives the love that was meant for her intended spouse to another man and joins with him, either openly or in secret, then she must not only abandon all hope of receiving any of her fiancé's promises, but she justly deserves the blame and sanction of the law.[1] It is just the same with us. If someone transfers his love of Christ the bridegroom to a desire for any other thing, either openly or in secret, and his heart becomes enthralled with it, then such a man will be hateful and abominable to the bridegroom and unworthy to be united with him, for he has said: 'I love those who love me.'[2]

3.53. For those who have this pledge, it is something ineffable, understood in a way beyond understanding, held without being contained, visible without being seen. It is something that lives and speaks and moves, and it moves whoever is holding it. It can be locked in a chest and disappear, and then unexpectedly be found again inside. This is so its owner may never think that it is here to stay or gone forever. In this way he realizes that not having it is just like having it, and having it is just like not having it.

3.54. Suppose a man were to stand inside a house at night with all the doors shut. He opens a window, and suddenly a flash of lightning wraps him round in its brilliance. His eyes cannot bear the flash so he immediately protects himself, closing his eyes and falling back. It is the same with the soul enclosed in the senses. If it leans outside, as if through the window of the mind,[1] it is dazzled by the lightning-flash of the pledge within it (I am speaking of the Holy Spirit) and it cannot bear the radiance of this unbearable light. It is immediately struck with amazement[2] and falls back totally on

---

3.52.[1] Under Byzantine law, if a betrothed person married someone other than the partner stated in the contract, this union was considered a second marriage.

3.52.[2] Prov 8:17.

3.54.[2] Cf. Ps 48:5 (LXX).

3.54.[1] Cf. Sg 2:9.

itself, taking refuge in its own house within sensible and human forms.

3.55. From such signs as these, every man should consider whether he has received the pledge of the Spirit from Christ our bridegroom and master. If he has received it, let him strive to preserve it. If he has not yet deserved to receive it, let him strive to receive it through good works and deeds and fervent repentance. Then let him guard it through the practice of the commandments and the acquisition of the virtues.

3.56. The roof of any house stands upon the foundations and the rest of the structure. The foundations themselves are laid in order to carry the roof. This is both useful and necessary, for the roof cannot stand without the foundations and the foundations are absolutely useless without the roof — no help to any living creature. In the same way the grace of God is preserved by the practice of the commandments, and the observance of these commandments is laid down like foundations through the gift of God. The grace of the Spirit cannot remain with us without the practice of the commandments, but the practice of the commandments is of no help or advantage to us without the grace of God.

3.57. If a lazy builder has left the house without a roof, it is not only useless, but it also makes a laughing-stock of the builder. In the same way a man may lay down the foundations of the commandments and raise up the walls of the higher virtues, but if he does not receive the grace of the Spirit in the contemplation and knowledge of his soul, he is imperfect and an object of pity to the perfect. This [grace] can be utterly refused to him for two reasons: either he neglects to repent or else, by retreating before the ranks of virtues as if they were an endless host, he may have missed one of them out. It may seem to be the most insignificant, but it is really so essential for the completion of this house of the virtues that without it, it cannot be roofed over by the grace of the Spirit.

3.58. The Son of God, God himself, came upon the earth so that we who were his enemies might be reconciled to his Father through him,[1] and consciously joined with him through his holy and consubstantial Spirit. If, then, a man misses this grace what other shall he obtain? He will not be reconciled to him or united with him through participation in the Spirit.

3.59. The sage said: 'Who can bring fire to his bosom and not burn his garments?'[1] but I say: Who can receive the unbearable heavenly fire in his heart without being set alight and illumined; without radiating the lightning flashes of the very deity in proportion to his purification and participation in this fire? For participation comes with this purification, and when they meet our purification results. When this happens, man becomes entirely God by grace.

3.60. When a man participates in the Holy Spirit he is delivered from passionate desires and pleasures, but he is not exempted from the bodily necessities of our nature. When he is freed from these chains of passionate appetites and inflamed by immortal glory and delight, he is urged on ceaselessly to be up above and to live with God. He never leaves aside this contemplation and insatiable joy even for an instant. But when he is fettered by the body and by corruption, he is pulled down, dragged along, and turned back to the things of earth. Then he feels such grief as I think the sinner must feel when his soul is separated from the body.

3.61. When a man loves his body, his life, and this world along with all its pleasures, it would be death for him to be separated from them. And in the same way when a man loves holiness, divinity, immateriality, and virtue, then it is death for him if his thoughts should even be slightly separated from these things. A man can look upon the sensible light, but if he closes his eyes for an instant or if someone else covers them up, he is distressed and afflicted and wholly unable to bear it.

3.58.[1] Rom 5:10.   3.59.[1] Prov 6:27.

This applies all the more if he were looking at something important or wonderful. How much more, then, does it apply to the man who is illumined in the Holy Spirit, who sees intelligibly without illusion, whether waking or sleeping, the good things which the eye has not seen nor ear heard, which have not entered into the heart of man,[1] things which even the angels long to glimpse.[2] If anyone, then, should tear him away from this contemplation, would he not be grieved and distressed? It would seem like death to him, a veritable exclusion from eternal life.

3.62. Man is two-fold,[1] composed of soul and body, and like him the world has been made visible and invisible. To each of these aspects correspond harmoniously our works and our care for these works. From this I believe we can draw a true inference about dreams and visions. What occupies the soul here, and enters it while it is awake, still occupies its imagination and thoughts during sleep. The soul is still engaged in human affairs even though its imagination is then occupied by dreams. It may even meditate on divine and heavenly realities, and then it enters into visions and reflects on apparitions just as the prophet said: 'Their young men shall see visions.'[2] The soul is not deceived; it perceives truths and can rely on these revelations.

3.63. When the concupiscible part of the soul is roused to passion, intercourse, and the joys and pleasures of life, the soul sees these same things in its dreams. If the irascible element makes it angry with its fellows, it dreams of the assaults of wild animals, of battles and struggles with serpents, and it argues with its opponents as if in front of a tribunal. If its rational faculty is puffed up by vanity or pride, the soul fancies that it has wings and flies in the air, or else sits on a high throne, or marches at the head of a people in front of a column of chariots.

3.61.[1] 1 Cor 2:9.   3.62.[1] Cf. *Chapters* 2:23.
3.61.[2] 1 Pet 1:12.   3.62.[2] Joel 3:1.

3.64. Yet the only true apparitions (and then we must call them not dreams, but visions and contemplations) come to those whose minds are made simple by the indwelling of the Spirit and free from all hindrance or slavery of the passions. All their curiosity goes on divine things, and their reflections on the future recompense and retribution. Their life, more than any other life, is without care or anxiety. It is calm, pure, full of mercy, wisdom, heavenly knowledge, and the good fruits cultivated by the Spirit. But as for those who are not like this and do not have these characteristics, theirs is a lying vision, confused and patently fallacious.

3.65. Many people hold the eremitical life in high esteem, others the common or the cenobitic life, and others the governance of the people, or education and teaching, or the administration of churches. Different persons earn their bodily and spiritual sustenance in all these ways. For myself, I cannot judge in favor of any one of these states. I would not exalt one kind and deprecate another. In any case, whatever our works or activities, the most blessed life of all is one that is [lived] for God and according to God in each single act and deed we do.

3.66. Human life is made up of different sciences and arts, and each of them can be seen to practise its own specialty and make its own contribution. So it is that we men live and meet the physical needs of our nature, sometimes contributing to others and sometimes receiving from them. It is just the same with spiritual men: one practises one virtue, and someone else another. They follow two different ways of life, but by both they run to the same goal.

3.67. For all those who engage in God's struggle, the goal is to be pleasing to Christ our God and to receive our reconciliation with the Father through communion in the Spirit. This is how we attain our salvation, for it is the salvation of each soul and every man. If we do not win, then all our effort is empty and our work is in vain. And any way of life that does not lead the runner to this end is equally futile.

3.68. Suppose a man abandons the whole world to go far off in the mountains for spiritual stillness,[1] but then starts to write pretentiously to those who are still in the world, blessing some and flattering and praising others. He is just like a man who has married a debauched woman, slatternly and utterly wicked, and has then gone far away to rid himself even of her memory. But when he arrives at the mountain he forgets why he has come, and wants to write to those who still hang round this prostitute, as it were, and pollute themselves with her; and he blesses them! This man has exactly the same passion in his intentions as all the others—if not in body then certainly in heart and mind—because he approves of their dealings with her.

3.69. Those who live in the midst of the world deserve praise and blessings when they purify their hearts and senses from all evil desires. But to the same degree, if those who dwell in the mountains and caves[1] seek the praises, blessings, and glory of men, they should be blamed and cast off as worthless. They shall be as adulterers to the God who searches our hearts. [Any man who wants his life or name or career to make a great noise in the world prostitutes himself away from God, just as the Jewish people did in ancient times, as David tells us.[2]

3.70. When a man renounces the world and all that is in the world with a steadfast faith in God, he believes that the Lord is merciful and compassionate, and welcoming all who come to him in repentance. Yet he is aware that he honors his servants with dishonor, enriches them with abject poverty, glorifies them through insults and abuse, and restores them to their heritage and participation in eternal life by means of

3.68.[1] *Hesychia*: see *Chapters* 1.95.
3.69.[1] Cf. Heb 11:38.   3.69.[2] Ps 106:39.

death. By all these means the man races onwards to the immortal fountain like a thirsting deer, and he uses them all to climb the heights as if he were on a ladder where the angels ascend and descend[1] to help those who climb. God waits on high, watching over our zeal and whatever efforts we are able to make, not because he delights in seeing us suffer, but because he is the lover of man and wants to give us rewards as if they were our due.

3.71. When people go to the Lord with a firm resolve, he never allows them to fall back completely. He sees their weakness and works with them to help. He stretches out his hand of power from on high and draws them to himself. His assistance is at the same time open, yet secret, conscious, yet unconscious, until such time as we have climbed right up the ladder and drawn close to him. Then we will be made one in the All and forget all the things of earth, and be with God, whether in body or out of it I do not know.[1] There we shall be fellow citizens, enjoying the good things that cannot be described.

3.72. It is only right that our first step should be to take the yoke of Christ's commandments on our shoulders. We should neither kick nor drag behind, but go forward in these things straightly and surely until our death. We should transform ourselves into the new paradise of God,[1] until such time as the Son with the Father enters us through the Holy Spirit and dwells within. Then, when we possess him completely as our guest and teacher, he can command any of us, no matter how great may be the task with which he entrusts us, and we shall simply stretch out our hand to it and accomplish it with all eagerness just as he intended. But it is not right to look for this before the proper time or to accept it from the hands of men. No, we must abide in the commandments of our God and master and wait expectantly for his instructions.

3.70.[1] Cf. Gen 28:12, Jn 1:51.
3.71.[1] 2 Cor 12:2.   3.72.[1] Cf. *Ethical Discourse* 2:8.

3.73. If we have undertaken to serve in divine things and have excelled in them, then if the Spirit commands us to turn to a different kind of service, work, or activity, we must not resist. God does not wish us to be idle or to remain until the end in the selfsame activity in which we started out. He wants us to progress and always to be ready to move on to the attainment of greater things. We must march along in step with God's will, not ours.

3.74. When a man has killed off his own will, he becomes altogether devoid of will. And yet, apart from what we might call insensible and immobile objects, there is no being that lives and moves which is without a will. In the case of plants, even though they move and grow, we still do not say that they move and grow by natural volition, because they are devoid of soul. But every creature that has a soul also has a natural will. So then, when a man has put his self-will to death by fervent ascesis and become completely devoid of will, it follows that he must have left his own proper nature behind. Since he no longer wills, he can perform neither good nor evil.

3.75. When a man strives to mortify his self-will he should submit to God's will. Instead of his own will, he should introduce God's, and implant and graft this onto his heart. To help him in this he should take a close look at plants and grafted shoots. The former flourish by pushing down deep roots, the latter scar over and join together, becoming one with the trees. If they grow and flourish they bear a beautiful sweet fruit, and you would never be able to recognize in it the ground in which it was sown or the root on which it was grafted. This plant is a living mystery which words cannot express.

3.76. When the fear of God leads a man to eradicate his own will, God mysteriously graces him in an incomprehen-

3.76.¹ Mk 4:27.

sible way[1] with the divine will, and preserves it indelibly in his heart. He opens the eyes of his mind to recognize it and gives him strength to accomplish it. The grace of the Holy Spirit brings all these things to effect, and nothing at all happens without it.[2]

3.77. When we have accomplished the things which God himself has mystically and mysteriously taught us; when we have done them with all our strength, with eagerness, purpose and unflagging zeal, without neglecting anything at all that he has instructed, then we receive a clear revelation. This is given to us because we have been faithful and obedient, his true disciples and friends, and just as in ancient times it was revealed to his holy disciples and apostles and to all who through them believed in his name,[1] so it is to us. Then we become sons of God by grace, as Paul said, 'All those who are led by the Spirit of God are sons of God, and if they are sons they are also heirs, heirs of God and co-heirs of Christ.[2]

3.78. Those whom God has deemed worthy to be with him in the communion of the Spirit and taste his good things that cannot be expressed, no longer have any love for the low and tawdry glory that men offer, whether it be gold, or garments or those stones which madmen think are precious. Such a man does not set his heart on riches which are always shifting,[1] and has no desire to be recognized by kings or rulers. The latter, in fact, do not really rule at all, but are ruled by the mob. He does not think there is anything great or eminent about these people, or that their closest courtiers have any greater glory. And in the same way that any other man would strive to avoid falling from riches to poverty or from the first and highest authority or coveted dignity into the lowest dishonor or disgrace, so does this man strive to have no desire for anything at all that men consider outstanding or brilliant.

3.76.[2] Cf. Jn 1:3.   3.77.[2] Rom 8:14, 17.
3.77.[1] Jn 17:20.   3.78.[1] Cf. Ps 62:10.

3.79. If you have received the remission of your sins through confession or through clothing in the holy and angelic habit, it should be a great occasion of love and thanksgiving and humility for you. For even though you have earned a thousand punishments, you have not only been released, but have even gained sonship, glorification, and the kingdom of heaven. Meditate on these things and ponder them always, and be ready and careful never to dishonor him who has honored you and forgiven you a thousand faults. In all that you do give him glory and honor,[1] so that he may in return glorify you[2] all the more. He has already honored you above all visible creation, and he will call you his true friend.[3]

3.80. Just as the soul is more precious than the body, so the rational man is superior to the whole world. So when you reflect on the immensity of all the creatures that are in it, do not think that they are more precious than you. Think about the grace which has been given to you, and recognize the dignity of your soul, endowed with intelligence and reason. Then you will sing praise to the God who has honored you above all visible creation.

3.81. Let us examine how we glorify God. The only possible way we can glorify him is the way in which he has been glorified by the Son, for in the same way that the Son glorified his Father, the Father glorified him.[1] We too should diligently use these same means to glorify him who has condescended to be called our Father in heaven so that we might be glorified by him in the glory of Jesus which he had with the Father before ever the world was.[2] These means are the (cross) (I mean dying to the whole world), trials, temptations, and all the other sufferings of Christ. If we bear these things with great patience, we are then imitating the sufferings of

3.79.[1] Cf. 1 Cor 10:31.   3.81.[1] Jn 17:1.
3.79.[2] Cf. Jn 17:1.   3.81.[2] Jn 17:5.
3.79.[3] Jn 15:15.

Christ and using them to glorify our God and Father as his sons by grace, the co-heirs of Christ.

3.82. When a soul does not sense its perfect liberation from reliance and attachment to visible reality, it cannot bear the troubles and insults which come to it, whether from demons or men, without feeling grief. It is like a prisoner of its passion for the things of men. It is afflicted when it loses money, suffers when it is deprived, and tortured if wounds are inflicted on its body.

3.83. If a man has snatched his soul away from the possession and desire of sensible realities and fixed it on God, he will not only despise all the wealth and goods that surround him and remain indifferent to their loss as if they were the property of strangers, but he will even bear with joy and proper thanksgiving the sufferings which fall on his body. Such a man always has before his eyes what the divine apostle spoke of: the outer man who is perishing and the inner man who is renewed from day to day.[1] If this were not the case it would be impossible to bear with joy any of these tribulations which God has allowed. To do so, a man needs perfect understanding and spiritual wisdom, and if he does not have these, he will always walk in the darkness of ignorance and despair, completely unable to see the light of patience and consolation.

3.84. No pseudo-Solomon of the mathematical sciences is ever found worthy to see revealed the mysteries of God until he has first agreed to humble himself and become as a fool,[1] rejecting all his self conceit and even the knowledge he already possesses. If he does this, and follows after divine things with unshakable faith in the company of the wise, then he will enter the city of the living God hand in hand with them. He will be guided and illumined by the divine Spirit, and will see and learn things which no other man has looked upon or can ever see or learn. He will then be taught by God himself.[2]

3.83.[1] 2 Cor 4:16.   3.84.[1] 1 Cor 3:18.   3.84.[2] Jn 6:45.

3.85. Those who are taught by God are considered morons by the disciples of the wise men of this age, but it is really they who are the fools. It is they who are gagged by this foolish wisdom which God himself has made foolish according to the divine apostle.[1] His inspired voice recognized it as something earthly, carnal, demonic, full of jealousy and contradiction.[2] Men like this are outside the divine light and cannot see the wonders within it. They think that those who live in the light, and see and learn the things it contains, are misguided, but it is they who are misguided, they who have never tasted the ineffable gifts of God.

3.86. This is why those who are filled with grace, who are perfect in knowledge and wisdom from above, have only one reason for wishing to venture out and look upon those who are in the world. It is so that they can bring them some advantage by reminding them of God's commandments and good works. It might just be that they will listen, and even understand and be convinced. Yet all those who are not led by the Spirit of God[1] walk in the darkness. They do not know where they are going[2] or what they have stumbled over. Perhaps when they recover from the self-conceit that hems them in they will truly receive the teaching of the Holy Spirit. Perhaps they will hear the will of God without error or deception, and repent. Perhaps they will put it into practice and receive some spiritual gift in return. If, however, the mediators cannot win this benefit for them, then they lament the hardness of their hearts and retire again to their wooden huts, praying night and day for their salvation. For those who are ceaselessly in union with God and brimming over with every good, this is the only thing that causes them sorrow.

3.87. Even now there are those who are impassible, saints full of the divine light, who live in our midst. They have so

3.85.[1] 1 Cor 1:20.
3.85.[2] Jas 3:15.

3.86.[1] Rom 8:14.
3.86.[2] Jn 12:35.

mortified their earthly members[1] from all impurity and passionate desires that they never think of evil themselves, and no one else could ever lead them into doing it. Yet there are men who accuse these saints of folly, and do not believe them when they teach the things of God in the wisdom of the Spirit. This transformation into impassibility takes place before their very eyes, and they would have understood it if they had only grasped the divine sayings that are read each day and chanted in their presence. If they had achieved a perfect understanding of the divine scriptures they would have believed in the good things God has spoken about and given to us. Yet their self-conceit and carelessness prevent them from having any share in these beautiful things, and they accuse those who do share them and teach about them, and they refuse to believe them.

3.88. The purpose of the incarnate economy of God the Word, which is proclaimed by all the divine scriptures and which we read but do not understand, is surely summed up by saying that he has shared in what was ours to let us share in what was his.[1] The Son of God became the Son of Man in order to make us men the sons of God. By grace he lifts up our race to what he is by nature. He gives birth to us from on high in the Holy Spirit, and then straightway leads us into the kingdom of heaven; or rather, he gives us the grace to have this kingdom within us.[2] We therefore have more than just the hope of entering here; we really possess it as we cry out: 'Our life is hidden with Christ in God.'[3]

3.89. Baptism does not take away our self-determination or our free will; instead, it grants us freedom no longer to be held against our will in the devil's tyranny. For after baptism it is up to us to decide to remain in the commandments of Christ, our master, into which we were baptized and to walk

3.87.[1] Col 3:5.   3.88.[2] Lk 17:21.
3.88.[1] Cf. 2 Pet 1:4.   3.88.[3] Col 3:3.

in the way of his ordinances,[1] or else to deviate from the right path by evil deeds and to run back to our adversary and enemy, the devil.

3.90. If men give way to the wishes of the evil one after their baptism and put these decisions into effect, they cut themselves off from the holy womb of baptism in accordance with the saying of David.[1] But no one can become something else or change his nature. It has been fixed from creation itself. Each man is created good by God because God has never made evil. Each is created unchangeable in nature and essence. Each chooses and decides whatever seems right in his own judgement, either for good or for evil. Whether a sword be used for good or for evil does not change its proper nature: it remains steel. And it is the same when a man stirs into action, as I have said; he does what he wills, but he does not change his own nature.

3.91. If we have pity on one man it does not save us, but to despise even one man sends us to the flames. The saying: 'I was hungry and thirsty'[1] was not given for one single occasion or meant just for one day; it sets out the whole course of life. To feed Christ, then, or to give him drink, or clothes, or whatever else is mentioned, is not something done once and once alone, it is something our Lord and God has told us he receives from his servants through all and in all.

3.92. Christ is divided without being divided, and complete in each one of the poor. How then can some people lock him up in a single poor man? Imagine a hundred poor persons; there is only one Christ, for Christ is in no way divided.[1] So if someone gives pennies to each of the ninety-nine, but strikes or maltreats the last one, or sends him away without anything, then he is doing all these things to the one who said, and says through all ages, and will always say:

3.89.[1] Cf. 1 Kgs 8:61.   3.91.[1] Mt 25:35.
3.90.[1] Ps 58:3.   3.92.[1] Cf. 1 Cor 1:13.

'Each time you did this for one of the least of these, you did it for me.'[2]

3.93. If a man who has given alms to a hundred can still give to others to supply them with food and drink, but instead sends them all away[1] in spite of their shouts and cries, he shall be judged before Christ as having refused him comfort. Since Christ himself is in all these, as we feed the least of them, we feed him.

3.94. If one day a man supplies the needs of everyone, but on the next day neglects some of his brothers, although he could still help, and leaves them to perish from hunger and thirst and cold, then he has scorned and allowed to die him who said: 'Whenever you did this for one of the least of these, you did it for me.'

3.95. We can learn something from all this: that the Lord makes everything to do with our poor brothers his personal concern. For he says to the just: 'You did it for me', and to those on the left he says: 'You did not do it for me.' He does not consider only those we have treated compassionately when they have been wounded and injured or borne a thousand other sufferings, he also looks at those we neglected, and this is enough to condemn us because it was not they whom we neglected, but he who made all their affairs his very own, Jesus the Christ.

3.96. If He has condescended to assume the features of each poor man and make himself like all the poor, it is so that none of his faithful should ever raise himself above his brother, but that each one should look on his brother and his neighbor as his very God and consider himself the least of all, not in regard to his neighbor, but to his Maker. We must therefore welcome [our brother] as [Christ]. We should honor him and put all our resources at his disposal, just as Christ and God emptied out his own blood for our salvation.

3.92.[2] Mt 25:40.   3.93.[1] Cf. Mt 14:15.

3.97. When we are commanded to consider our neighbor as ourself,[1] this does not mean for just one day, but all through life. When a man is told to give to all who ask,[2] he is told to do this for all of his days. If a man wants people to do good to him, he himself will be required to do good to others.[3]

3.98. When a man really considers his neighbor as himself, he will never tolerate having more than his neighbor. If he does have more, but refuses to share things generously until he himself becomes as poor as his neighbor, then he will find that he has not fulfilled the commandment of the master. He no longer wants to give to all who ask, and instead turns away from someone who asks of him while he still has a penny or a crust of bread. He has not treated his neighbor as he would like to be treated by him.[1] In fact, even if a man had given food and drink and clothes to all the poor, even the least, and had done everything else for them, he has only to despise or neglect a single one and it will be reckoned as if he had passed by Christ and God when He was hungry and thirsty.

3.99. All this may perhaps seem very harsh to most people, and it will seem reasonable for them to say: 'Who can possibly do all this,[1] feeding and caring for everybody so that no one is left out?' But they should listen to Paul, who specifically says: 'The love of Christ constrains us when we consider that if one man has died for all, then all men have died.'[2]

3.100. The universal commandments contain all the particular commandments, and in the same way the universal virtues embrace the particular virtues. When a man sells all he has and gives to the poor, he becomes poor himself at one stroke, and he has fulfilled all the requirements of the particular commandments in one act. He no longer needs to give to those who ask him, or drive away those who want to borrow

3.97.[1] Deut 6:5, Lk 10:26.   3.98.[1] Mt 7:12.
3.97.[2] Mt 5:42.   3.99.[1] Cf. Mt 19:25.
3.97.[3] Mt 7:13.   3.99.[2] 2 Cor 5:14.

from him.[1] It is the same for the man who practises continuous prayer. He has encompassed everything else within this, and no longer needs to praise the Lord seven times a day[2] with morning, midday, and evening prayers.[3] He has already fulfilled all the canonical prayers and hymns at the appointed times and hours.[4] And when a man knows that he has within him the God who gives men knowledge, he has passed through all the holy Scriptures; and because he has picked all the fruit of his reading, he no longer needs to read the books. How is this? Well, if the same One who inspired the scriptural writers abides within this man as his intimate, and initiates him into the secrets of the hidden mysteries, then he himself becomes a divinely inspired book for others. He bears the new and ancient[5] mysteries inscribed in him by the finger of God,[6] for he has fulfilled all things and rests from all his labors[7] in God who is the supreme perfection.

The end of the 225 Chapters.

3.100.[1] Cf. Mt 5:42.   3.100.[2] Ps 119:64.   3.100.[3] Ps 55:17.
3.100.[4] See St Basil, *Regulae brevius tractatae*; PG 31:1113.
3.100.[5] Cf. Mt 15:32.   3:100.[6] Ex 31:18.   3.100.[7] Gen 2:2.

THE THREE
THEOLOGICAL DISCOURSES

THE FIRST THEOLOGICAL DISCOURSE

AGAINST THOSE WHO ASCRIBE THE CONCEPT OF
ANTERIORITY TO THE FATHER

IT WOULD BE THE SIGN of a rash and presumptuous
soul to speak or discourse about God, to investigate all
that concerns him, or to try to express what cannot be
expressed, or understand what for all men is beyond understanding. This is not only the affliction of those who take it
upon themselves to talk about God, but even those who try
to repeat the sayings of the theologians who have been in-
spired by God, |sayings| with which they fought the here-
tics in times past and which have been handed on to us in
writing. Such persons interpret these in every conceivable
sense, not in order to gain spiritual profit, but to be admired
by their audience at banquets and gatherings, and in order to
make a name for themselves as theologians. It saddens and
disturbs me, especially when I think of the terrible trial and
judgement which awaits such foolhardy men. What presumptuous statements they have made about God!

According to my opponent,[1] the only reason that the
Father is greater than the Son[2] is that he is the cause of the
Son's existence. To this I reply: 'In what way are you saying
that the Father is greater than the Son?'. And he answers:
'The Father is clearly greater than the Son, or in other words
"anterior", because the Son is from the Father'. Such are the
vain novelties which their senseless theology proclaims. They
do not know the reasons why the theologians spoke in this
way against the heretics. Unable to grasp the true sense of
the writings, they stumble blindly on and present their own
interpretations as if they were assured truth, real and certain.

1. An unknown opponent, possibly Stephen the *Synkellos*.
2. Jn 14:28.

To men like this we do not speak as from ourselves, we rely on the Spirit who makes himself heard from above, and we speak as the initiates of him who teaches men knowledge.[3] Now let us speak.

If the all-holy trinity who has drawn the universe from non-being always was, is now, and always will be indivisible, then tell me who among you has taught or conceived these measures and degrees within it? This 'first' and 'second', this 'greater' and 'lesser'? Who has set this out so clearly with regard to the invisible and unknown |hypostases], who are absolutely beyond thought and speech? Since they are eternally united and eternally unchanging they cannot have any priority among themselves. If you want to say that the Father is prior to the Son because the Son is born from him, and for this reason is also greater, then I for my part say to you that the Son is prior to the Father, for if the Son had not been born then the Father would not have been called 'Father.' If, |on the other hand|, you place the Father altogether before the Son, and categorize him as prior in that he is the cause of the Son's generation, then I also reject |the idea| that he is the 'cause' of the Son. For in this way you allow it to be implied that before the Son was begotten he did not exist, and that he was begotten according to whether he willed it or not, or whether the Father willed it or not, and that he could have known or have been ignorant about his generation and the manner in which it was to take place. You see what paradoxes, not to say blasphemies, into which these inquiries make us fall? So you must either renounce the expression 'the Father is prior to the Son', in which case we will admit what you say about the Father as the cause, or if you insist on the first expression even after we have placed it under judgement,[4] then we must equally reject your second. As we have said, they are eternally united and eternally unchanging, so they cannot be the cause of one another.

---

3. Ps 94:10.   4. Ps 112:5 (lxx).

If you do not imagine that the Father existed before the Son, you will not be led to say that he is prior to, or greater than, the Son. A being which pre-exists can be said to be prior to that which it has engendered, produced, or created, but how can he be spoken of as prior to the co-eternal? The Son is himself eternal and without beginning, just as the Father is. The Father, then, does not pre-exist, and never has been and never will be prior to the Son. On the contrary, he is complete in the complete and equally glorious Son, just as the Son is in the complete and consubstantial Father. If you say that the Father is the cause of the Son, then I must point out that you imply there was a time when God was alone, when the Son was not,[5] and that he engendered him later and thus became the cause of his existence. This is impiety and leads you far from God and the truth. It puts you in the ranks of the ungodly who say that the Son is a creature of the Father. Even to think this is the height of impiety and atheism.

We say that the Father is the cause of the birth of the Son in regard to his bodily generation,[6] but as to that divine subsistence which is without subsistence, the birth which is unborn, the substance which is not substance, and the essence beyond all essence[7] (or whatever else there is beyond my intellect), then if anyone talks about a first he must also refer to a second and a third. This manner of speaking cannot apply in any way to the all-holy Trinity. What a foolish and dangerous undertaking it would be to measure out the immeasurable or to speak of the ineffable or to discourse about that which is beyond words. So with regard to the divine and ineffable generation of God the Word, we say that the Father is the cause of the Son just as the mind is of the spoken

5. This was the fourth-century Arian catchword. Symeon is characterizing his opponents as new Arians.

6. Cf. John of Damascus, *De fide orthodoxa*; PG 94:820B.

7. Symeon here adopts the language of the mystical tradition deriving from Pseudo-Dionysius.

word or the spring of the stream, or root of branches, but we do not say that he is prior, in case we multiply the number or divide the one indivisible deity into three gods.

In this trinity which is without any division or confusion, one cannot conceive or speak about a first, a second, or a third, or about a great or a small. It is absolutely impossible to speak or express or even conceive the properties of a divine nature which is above and beyond all essence. The human mind simply cannot comprehend it. But if you still want to exercise your reason in a different way and learn how incomprehensible is that God who gave being to all things from non-being, then let us suppose you were to place the Spirit in front of the Son and the Father (what a way for a theologian to speak!). In this case, you will find in him the complete identity of the co-eternal persons because they are consubstantial. You see how the properties of the divine nature are incomprehensible for us men? It is said that 'God is Spirit'[8] and again that 'The Lord is the Spirit'.[9] So if God is Spirit and the Lord is the Spirit, where here is that Fatherhood or Sonship which makes you modern theologians teach and propose and enumerate a first and a greater in that divine and incomprehensible nature?

John the Theologian said, 'In the beginning was the Word',[10] not | 'in the beginning was| the Father'. Have you |theologians| received from Jesus, who is Wisdom itself, an initiation even more profound than John's, that you can propose for us and the whole world the concept of the Father as first, that you can show the Son to be second after him, and the Holy Spirit in his turn a third? You are preaching a different Gospel to us.[11] You pass yourselves off as theologians more profound than the ancients and more intimate with the Son of God. What blasphemy! Since you perversely teach us the doctrine of tritheism, tell us then why the Theologian who rested on the breast of Christ did not say: 'In the begin-

8. Jn 4:24.   9. 2 Cor 3:17.   10. Jn 1:1.   11. Gal 1:6.

ning was the Father', but 'In the beginning was the Word';
and why did he say 'Word' and not 'Son', except to teach us
that no one knew there was a Son, or that God was a Father,
until God the Word descended and became incarnate? This
is not to say that the three-personed Godhead, source of all
that is, did not yet exist, but only that the mystery of the incarnation was as yet unknown. For it is only after the incarnation of God the Word that God the Father was also known
by us believers as a Father, and that God the Word, who became incarnate for our sake, was known as the Son of God,
in accordance with that word which the Father spoke from
heaven: 'This is my beloved Son, listen to him'.[12] And the
Son said: 'Righteous Father, the world has not known you
but I have known you';[13] and again: 'I have made your name
known to men';[14] and again: 'Father, glorify your Son that
your Son may glorify you';[15] and finally: 'I and the Father
are one'.[16] If, then, the Son and the Father are one after the
incarnation of God the Word, how much more so before the
incarnation!

Consider carefully with me the force of these words. He
says: 'I and the Father are one'. Why does he name himself
before the Father? It is in order to show us that he himself is
absolutely equal to the Father in dignity and glory, and that
the Father is not first even though he is the cause of the Son,
nor is the Son second even though he comes from the Father,
nor is the Holy Spirit third even though he proceeds from
the Father. If the Trinity is one from the very beginning and
is called a trinity in regard to the persons, then it follows that
one cannot in any way be prior either to himself or to the
other persons with him. The one did not pre-exist the other
so that by virtue of this pre-existence he is prior to the bright-
ness born from him. There is but one Godhead, one Trinity,
and, as I have said, it is called such with regard to the persons

| 12. Mt 17:5. | 14. Jn 15:15. | 16. Jn 10:30. |
| 13. Jn 17:25. | 15. Jn 17:1. | |

and hypostases. But because it is divided without division and united without confusion God is called a single trinity. No one [of the persons] has ever pre-existed the others so that one becomes prior to another, not the Father in relation to the Son, nor the Son to the Father, nor both of them in relation to the Spirit. They have a simultaneous beginning which is coeternal and without origin.

The Trinity is therefore one God; inexpressible, without beginning, uncreated, incomprehensible, undivided, and beyond all human thought or speech. But in case too long a silence should lead us into the disaster or forgetting him entirely, and we live in the world as atheists,[17] it has been granted to us to speak of God and the things of God so far as human nature allows, following the teachings of the divine apostles and our fathers inspired by God. Thus, by constantly renewing the memory of God, we glorify his goodness and the kindness he has shown us in the incarnation. We, who are dirt and ashes,[18] however, forget our true nature and stretch out to the limitless. We have no qualms about searching out the things that even angels and all the heavenly powers cannot understand or express. We analyze them as a pastime, categorize them, make up theories, and try to depict them all. In this we are no different from unbelievers or men who have never been initiated into the mysteries of Christ. This is how we think about the things of God, without the slightest feeling of awe, and we discourse on them in our presumption.

Since you have no fear in examining the divine nature, then tell me, do you believe that God is three persons without beginning, uncreated, incomprehensible, unsearchable, and invisible, that the mind cannot contain him, or words give expression to him, that he has been the self-same from all eternity, without any beginning of days or years or ages, and that he is eternally?[19] 'Of course,' you reply. But if you believe

17. Eph 2:12.   18. Gen 18:27.   19. Heb 7:3.

that the holy Trinity was one God alone, as indeed it was, and that when it so determined it drew the heavens and the earth and all they contain from non-being into being, created all the heavenly powers and then created man the last of all these, and [if you believe] that there is nothing in heaven or on earth or under the earth[20] which has not been drawn or produced from non-being, and that only God who made and created them all is uncreated, without beginning, existing eternally and before all things; well then, if you believe all this why do you not fall down in awe and silence before the world-maker as do all the powers of heaven? Why is it that you neglect to examine yourself, and try instead to discover his incomprehensible nature in your brash insolence? Have you no fear of lightning falling from heaven to consume you in its fire?

The one God in three persons is uncreated, without origin, existing eternally and before all things, and this consubstantial and indivisible trinity of one Godhead has produced all things visible and invisible, material and spiritual, known and unknown. As this is the case, tell me, then, if we were to compare all these things which have been made to the one who made them, how could such beings perceive his nature in any real way? It would be like comparing contingent things to the eternal existent, creatures to the uncreated, or temporal realities which have a dependent existence to the one who had no beginning. How could they perceive his immensity or the manner of his appearing? In no way at all! Except, that is, to the degree in which the maker of all creation, because of his love for man, himself gives to each the gift of knowing him as much as is expedient, just as he first gave him breath[21] and life and soul, intelligence and reason. If this were not so, how could we ever say that any being created by God would ever know its own creator?

Apart from this there is no means of arriving at [such

20. Ph 2:10.　　　21. Acts 17:25.

knowledge], and no one at all has the power to do so. But
the knowledge he has granted us believers is proportionate
to our faith, so that knowledge confirms faith independently
of knowledge, and that by this knowledge the man who has
heard the word and believed may, through this knowledge,
find confirmation that the teaching of the word has led him
to believe in one who is truly God. The faithful receive this
teaching by many different signs: by enigmas,[22] by mirrors,
in inexpressible mystic powers and divine revelations, by
veiled illuminations, by contemplation of the reasons of creation,[23] and many other means. In this way, their faith grows
day by day and rises up to the love of God. This is not all,
for God fills them, just as he did the apostles, through the
mission and presence of the Holy Spirit. They are enlightened more perfectly, and by this light they learn what it
means to say that God is ineffable and inexpressible, uncreated and eternal, endless and incomprehensible. Indeed, all
knowledge and discernment, every wise word and mystical
understanding, come to us only through the teaching of the
Spirit; so too the power of miracles, the gift of prophecy,
tongues, and interpretation,[24] the protection and government
of cities and peoples,[25] the knowledge of good things to come
and the attainment of the kingdom of heaven, the adoption
as sons,[26] the very putting on of Christ[27] and the knowledge
of the mysteries of Christ,[28] and the understanding of the
mystery of the economy in our regard. In short, we who
have been graced as believers are able to know and think and
speak about all these things which remain mysteries[29] to the
unbelievers.

  By these and similar means we are fully assured and convinced that it is God himself who has lifted the darkness of

22. 1 Cor 13:12.
23. For the platonic background to Symeon's terminology, see
Enneads 8.3.4.
24. 1 Cor 12:8-10.   26. Eph 1:5.   28. 1 Cor 14:2, Mt 13:11.
25. 1 Cor 12:28.   27. Rom 13:14.   29. Cf. Eph 3:1-5.

ignorance away from us; the same who made all things, who also created us by lifting us from the clay of the earth, who graced us with mind and reason and rational soul, who has made us in his own image and likeness.[30] It is he who has allowed us to see dimly realities which are beyond us, as though in a shadow, by analogy with the things that are at hand. From these things we have learned, and by them we see, and from them we believe, that just as he made our mind, our soul, and our immanent rationality at the same time he formed our bodies — for when we say that 'God formed man, taking clay from the earth, and breathed on his face the breath of life, and it became for him a living soul'[31] we show that our mind and reason existed at the same time as the soul; none of these pre-existed or was pre-supposed by the others, and the three together are one, and were given to us as one single breath of life — well, just as in this case none of the parts pre-existed or was pre-supposed by the others because there was a unity of essence and nature, so too none of the persons of the holy Trinity pre-existed the others since there is one and the same essence and glory. The three-personed God, the maker of the image,[32] never had one of the persons pre-existing the others. The three together are one very God, and in the same way the one is eternally three.

We therefore confess and believe this, and we witness to all others, that it is not rash to speak and inquire about the things of God, namely that God is three persons, Father, Son, and Holy Spirit, the holy Trinity in whose name we were baptized. We are assured of this by the powers and gifts of the Spirit which come down on us as well as by the sacred dogmas and the Gospels themselves. But as to how he is a Trinity, or since when, or what nature or origin he has who created all things, then we creatures simply do not know. And if we do not know, as in fact we do not, how many thunder-

30. Cf. Ps 40:2, Jb 10:9, Gen 1:26-7.
31. Gen 1:26.   32. Gen 2:7.

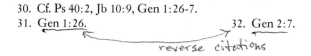

reverse citations

bolts would we deserve if we were to talk about something
we do not comprehend? We are visible creatures, corruptible and sensual, blind and devoid of light, how then can we
know something which is outside all created reality, whether
visible or invisible? In addition to this, our sins set up a dividing wall between God and ourselves and separate us from
him. If we do not destroy it or scale it through repentance,
we will not only be unable to know God, we will not even
know that we are men. While this partition stands, it cuts us
off from the light, and how can we possibly know ourselves
in the darkness of such a life? How could we truly know
what we are, or where we came from, or what our destiny is,
our origin and our end, or who we are? And if we do not
know ourselves, how much greater will be our ignorance of
him who is incomparably superior to us? If we were not
ignorant of ourselves we would not speak so rashly about
God. For to speak about God and divine things without illumination, while deprived of the Holy Spirit, simply shows
our ignorance about ourselves — and rightly so, for if we
knew ourselves accurately, we would never reckon ourselves
worthy to look at the heavens to see the light of this world,[33]
nor even to walk on the earth; instead, we would run to bury
ourselves under the dirt. Tell me, what more unclean thing
can there be than a man who in his presumptive pride tries
to teach the things of the Spirit without the Spirit? What is
more abominable than an unrepentant man who does not
purify himself beforehand, but neglecting this task tries to
theologize on the basis of a pseudo-knowledge[34] and a worldly wisdom? He speaks in utter insolence about those who
have existed from all ages in their self-identity. Even if there
were no other sin involved — which is impossible — this one
thing already places the man under an eternal judgement, for
'every proud man is unclean before the Lord.'[35]

Some of these men have come to ruin in such foolishness

33. Cf. Jn 11:9.   34. 1 Tim 6:20.   35. Prov 16:5.

because they would neither recognize nor confess that they
had sinned at all. What madness! No one is sinless save God
alone. The divine apostle says: 'All men have sinned and
fallen short of the glory of God, and are justified by the gift
of his grace.'[36] So, if according to this sacred Scripture, no
one is sinless save God alone[37] and all men have sinned and
fallen short of the glory of God, then anyone who says 'I
have not sinned' unwittingly makes himself the equal of
God, and is like the man who said 'I will place my throne
upon the clouds and I shall be like the Most High.'[38] But if
you confess that you have sinned, then show me the signs that
your confession is genuine: sincere trust in your spiritual
father who has received your thoughts, submission, obedience in servile works, care for your needy brothers, service
for the sick—and even more, profound humility of soul and
behavior without dissimulation, fraud, or pretence. Show me
that you have all these things in the inmost thoughts of your
soul, especially the dispositions that give rise to that constant
sorrow and the tears that bring joy, for it is in these and by
these that the zealous man gains the purification of his soul
and the knowledge of the mysteries of God. Only after all
this should you begin to speak about divine or human affairs.
Only then will I recognize the value of your words.

The fruit and role of repentance is at one and the same
time to dispel ignorance and obtain knowledge. I mean primarily knowledge about ourselves and human affairs, and
after this of things above us and of the divine mysteries which
are both invisible and incomprehensible to the unrepentant.
I am talking, of course, about [the mysteries] of our faith.
No man can win this treasure without the works I have just
mentioned, even if he were to go the whole round of philosophy. If a man has not become rich in the communion of this
[faith], he will spend his entire life in the deepest blackness
of ignorance. The divine matters and those which concern

36. Rom 3:23-4.   37. Lk 18:19, Jn 3:5.   38. Is 14:14.

the divinity are laid down in the Scriptures so that all men
can approach them for their own benefit, but they are only
revealed to those who have fervently repented and been purified by this sincere repentance; indeed, [the revelation] is in
due proportion to their repentance and purification. Only to
men like this are the depths of the Spirit revealed,[39] and they
in their turn present us with the word of the wisdom and
knowledge of God[40] from its very source. It is like an overflowing river which inundates the spirits of all that face it.
But for all other men these things remain unknown and hidden.[41] He who opens the minds of the faithful to the understanding of the Scriptures[42] never reveals them to such as
these, and rightly so, for it is said: 'My mystery is for me and
for mine.'[43] Thus, these men think that they see, but they do
not see; they think that they hear, but they hear nothing;
[they think] that they understand, but they are without
comprehension. They are unable to discern the things they
read. Each of the unbelievers thinks that he is reflecting
when he is not reflecting; he thinks he knows something but
he knows nothing at all; or if he does know something, he
knows it in a bad way which is worse than any ignorance.
And I think that these men are just the same. They think
that they are wise, but in fact have become unfortunate fools
who spend their days, as must be the case, like witless idiots
knowing nothing of the mysteries of Christ. May the God
of Israel deliver us from their presumption and pride and
grant that we may be considered worthy followers of his
own humility.[44]

Any man who leaves this path, then, and I mean [the path]
of blessed humility of spirit, placing his foot out of the way
and going on either to right or to left, and who does not fol-

39. 1 Cor 2:10.   41. Mt 13:13.
40. Rom 11:33, 1 Cor 12:8.   42. Lk 24:45.
43. This citation also appears in the work of Symeon's disciple Nicetas Stethatos; see *Opuscules et lettres*; SCh 81:280, and *Texte und
untersuchungen NF* 15.3-4 (Leipzig, 1916) p. 108.   44. Rom 1:22.

low the footsteps of Jesus our God, how can such a man enter
with him into the bridal chamber? And if he has not entered
with him, how will he contemplate his glory? And if he has
not contemplated it, how will he tell others what it is and
what it is like? How would he have the boldness to talk
about things he has never seen or understood? If he did try
to teach such awesome subjects would there be on earth any
more foolish man than he? Would he not be further removed
from reason than the beasts of the field, and even more bestial
than they, for at least the animals keep to the limits of their
own natures and stay within their own bounds. But such a
man, even though formed by the hand of God and honored
with reason and free will, has abused his position and failed to
recognize his own weakness. He has not remained in the
good things God put in his nature, and has neither stayed
within his own bounds nor even recognized his limitations.
No, like Lucifer and later Adam, the angel and the man who
rebelled against their Maker and pretended to be gods, this
man has sadly passed over the boundary of his own nature
and allowed himself to be carried away by fantasies and
desires for things beyond him. He has wished to scale the
heights of spiritual knowledge, not by Christ's example of
lowliness, but in arrogance and pride. This man has gathered
at random the bricks[45] of a pseudo-knowledge,[46] baked them
through assiduous meditation, and then assembled them into
a presumptuous edifice with one eye on the love of glory and
the other on pleasing his audience. He flatters himself that he
now possesses a tower of theology[47] and of spiritual knowledge. More than this, he even thinks that he is already in the
heavens or even above the heavens, and imagining that he
stands at their very summit, he discourses on the Creator of
heaven and earth and all that they contain. Could we call
such a creature a man? Who would rate him even as high as
the beasts? Who would credit him with any sense at all?

45. Gen 11:3.   46. 1 Tim 6:20.   47. Gen 11:4.

Man was made in the image of God and deemed worthy of
angelic and immortal life, but if he was rightly deprived of
that angelic state as well as of eternal life and condemned to
death, corruption, and the curse, all because he transgressed
that one commandment of God, then what will happen to
those of [Adam's] race who meddle in theology while they
still bear the image of dust[48] and have never been purified?
You are trying to meddle in the teachings about God and divine things, but you have never been taught yourself. Tell
me, have you first come up from hell to appear on earth?
How did you manage this? Through what steps and stages
did you make the ascent? Who helped you, and what manner of creature were they? You came to the surface stinking
and rotten with corruption, no more than a corpse in the
thrall of death. How did you lay hold on life again, overcome death, and succeed in escaping from his hands? Tell us
about these things and then, no doubt, you will tell us how
you managed to be delivered from your corruption and freed
from the curse after you came up from hell and arrived on
earth. After all this, you can show us how you were lifted up
from the earth. What kind of ladder did you use? What
kind of wings did you have to fly up to the highest heavens?
And in what kind of flesh did you rise up bodily so that you
could rise again outside that body[49] even higher? What cloud
lifted you up? Show us all these things and teach us on these
matters, and then we will recognize that you speak of God
legitimately, with fear and trembling.

But if a man rashly tried to preach without having manifested those spiritual signs which are always realized mystically in those who have reached the state of the completed
man in the measure of the stature of the fullness of Christ,[50]
or without having fulfilled the commandments of God, then I
would run from him as if he were a madman, a demoniac out
of his mind. Even Elijah was not lifted up to heaven bodily

48. 1 Cor 15:49.   49. 2 Cor 12:3.   50. Eph 4:13.

without the chariot of fire.[51] Even our God and master had the cloud of the Spirit to bear him up.[52] Nonetheless [God] could easily have carried Elijah from earth to heaven without the appearance of the chariot, as he did in the case of Enoch,[53] and the master himself could certainly have risen to the heavens on his own without the cloud or the escort of angels. But the fact is, he did not; and why? It was to teach us that our minds are completely dependent on someone to lift them up to heaven, and there to show them visions and reveal the mysteries of God. A bird cannot fly in the air without its wings; no more can the mind of man climb back to the place from which it fell without someone to guide it and lift it up high. And there is another reason, too, for the Master wanted to validate his own ascension and rising to heaven, as well as that of his servants, with the self-same works, and so teach us not to be deceived by mere words, nor to believe every man who claims to be spiritual, but to rely more on life and conduct, especially if a man's words and actions harmonize with the teachings of the Lord, the apostles, and the holy fathers. We should then receive and listen to his words as if they were the words of Christ himself. Otherwise even if a man were to raise the dead or show a thousand other miracles, run away from him and hate him as if he were a devil. You should do this all the more when it is obvious that in spite of warnings, he refuses to change his way of thinking and persists in his own perverted understanding, imagining that his way of life and behavior is heavenly.[54]

We have been initiated from on high by the inspired teaching of the apostles of Christ and our holy fathers, and we therefore reject the vain and empty voices of men who like nothing better[55] than ransacking and ferreting round things which are inaccessible even to the angels. Unshaking and steadfast, we hold fast to the confession of our faith[56] which

51. 2 Kgs 2:11. 53. Gen 5:24. 55. Cf. Acts 17:21.
52. Acts 1:9. 54. Cf. Phil 3:19. 56. Heb 4:14.

we have received from on high through them, a faith in the one Godhead, in Father, Son, and Holy Spirit, the unconfused and undivided Trinity into which we were baptized, by which we live, think, and understand, through which we continue to be and shall be evermore, which in wisdom drew the universe from non-being, from which we received our own existence and our well-being, and in the company of which we shall be able to pass from here below to the tranquil harbor of incorruptible life. For there is the dwelling place[57] of all those who are in joy, the place of all who celebrate in the Spirit, to whom be all glory, honor, and adoration, now and for ever, and through the ages of ages. Amen.

57. Ps 87:7.

THE SECOND THEOLOGICAL DISCOURSE

AGAINST THOSE WHO TRY TO THEOLOGIZE
WITHOUT THE SPIRIT

THE MAN WHO HAS RECEIVED from above the grace of having the praise of God always on his lips[1] opens his mouth to breathe the Spirit of life,[2] and strives to open it yet wider to welcome the word of life more abundantly. This is that bread coming down from heaven[3] of which it is said: 'Open wide your mouth and I shall fill it.'[4] Thus, when God has judged a man worthy to enter this state, he can have the consciousness of God impressed once and for all like a seal on the superior part of his soul[5] so that it is always present in his soul. And so, following the apostle's advice, whether he is eating or drinking,[6] he can rejoice always, pray ceaselessly, return thanks in every circumstance,[7] and refer all things to the glory of God. Truly, he is constantly fed and strengthened by this bread of life. When he sleeps, his heart keeps vigil,[8] and when he is awake, he is never in any way separated from God. This is what the apostle means when he says: 'He who joins himself to a woman forms one body, and he who unites himself with the Lord becomes one spirit.'[9] 'For God is spirit and those who worship him must worship in spirit and in truth.'[10] And it is also true that a man who is so united with God spiritually as to be one spirit with him is unable to sin, for the Theologian says: 'It is for this that the Son of God has appeared, to take away our sins. And there is no sin in him. Whoever abides in him does

1. Ps 34:1.
2. Ps 119:131.
3. Jn 6:50.
4. Ps 81:10.
5. *Hegemonikon.*
6. 1 Cor 10:31.
7. 1 Thess 5:17.
8. Sg 5:2.
9. 1 Cor 6:16.
10. Jn 4:24.

[123]

not sin,[11] and whoever sins has neither seen nor known him.'[12] Again: 'Whoever is born of God does not commit sin, for the divine seed abides within him and he cannot sin because he is born of God.'[13]

So if the man who sins has neither seen nor known God, and if anyone born of God does not commit sin because he is called the child [of God], then it amazes me why the majority of men should be at all afraid of theologizing or speaking about God, when they have been born of God and gained the title of children. For this reason, when I hear about some who philosophize on divine and inaccessible matters and theologize in a state of uncleanness and expound on God and what relates to him without the understanding which the Spirit gives, I tremble in spirit. I am beside myself! How incomprehensible is the Godhead! It is beyond thought or vision, and indeed, so are we to ourselves. We do not know what lies under our very feet! How is it, then, that we have nothing better to do than philosophize about God without the slightest fear? How can we speak so boldly about things which are inaccessible to us? We sin by the very fact that we speak about God, for all the while we are empty of the Spirit who illumines these things and reveals them to us.

It is hard for each man to know himself, and there are few who succeed in this philosophy. But small though it may be, this number will dwindle even more in our own time and in this generation when the love of philosophy is being blown out by the headwinds of prevailing apathy and [distracting] affairs of life. Men have exchanged eternal goods for those of no value, those which do not endure or which have no real existence at all because they are subject to change at the mercy of any circumstance and know no limit at which to

11. Symeon wishes to argue exegetically that the *natural* impeccability of Christ (*atreptos*) is communicated *by grace* to the believer. Cf. Gregory Nazianzen, *Orationes* 38:11; PC 26:344A; John of Damascus, PG 94:924A.

12. 1 Jn 3:8, 1 Jn 5:6.   13. 1 Jn 3.9.

stop. If this is so, how much more difficult it is to know God. Indeed, it is altogether contrary to reason and good sense to search out the nature and essence of God. So why do such men not repair their own house instead of searching out the things of God and all that concerns him? Our first concern should be to pass from death to life.[13] This is the condition for our receiving from on high the seed of the living God and of being begotten by him so as to be called his children. Only then do we draw the Spirit into our inmost being,[14] and by his illumination declare the things of God in the degree that this is possible, and according to the manner of our illumination by God.

For the present, if you wish to theologize about God in these terms, then I ask you to believe that God is one and alone, and that he has not been produced by any other, for nothing existed before him and nothing is older than he. This is not to say that he made himself, as some particularly foolish people have thought. It is impossible for non-being to pass of itself into being. No, he is from all eternity. He pre-exists and he will be forevermore one God in three persons. If you want to uphold the truth correctly, you should not say that something which exists as both one and three does not exist at all. Whoever learns about the things which transcend him from things which affect him will adore the One Godhead in three co-essential persons. And if he has not obscured or clouded the image through his passions, he will first of all recognize himself and know for a fact that the Creator has given him an immanent living soul constituted in three parts, for it includes mind and reason as well. And in this way, with a sure and clear conception, he will understand the things of God by analogy with the things that pertain to himself.

It is the Spirit who moves from on high that moves him on to an understanding of God the Father, he who has given

13. Jn 5:24.   14. Ps 51:10-12.

existence to the universe by drawing it from non-being by
his own word, and who by the power of his Spirit keeps it
together in being. It is he who, beyond all time, eternally
generates the Son who is of the same essence as he and who
is never separated from him; and with the Son and co-essential with him, the divine Spirit proceeds from the co-essential
Father. So it is that when a man has a correct conception of
God, he shows that he is himself the image of the Creator
whenever he makes a profession of faith, for he is endowed
with a soul that is reasonable, intelligent, and immortal, created by an intelligence and a reason which are co-essential
and indwelling. If it were otherwise, man would accuse himself of being totally devoid of intelligence and reason. If he
does away with these divine properties, then how, or in what
other way, or with what other qualities, is he to be the image
of the Creator? On the other hand, a man may admit he is
composed of such parts and correctly apply them to himself,
but then go against reason and deny their application to God,
the Creator upon whom he depends. Such a man would then
seem to me no different from a pagan — I dare not say from
the animals or reptiles and wild beasts.

For my part, this is what I believe: the soul did not take
precedence over or pre-exist intelligence, neither did intelligence [pre-exist] the reason it engenders. They received existence simultaneously from God. Intelligence gives birth to
reason and thereby produces the will of the soul. In the same
way, then, God the Father did not pre-exist the Son or the
Spirit. Just as intelligence is in the soul, having reason imma-
nently within itself, so too God the Father is in the entire Spirit, having entire in himself God the Word engendered. Just as
intelligence and reason cannot exist without the soul, so there
is no way of naming the Son and the Father apart from the
Holy Spirit. How could the living God exist without life?
It is the Holy Spirit which is the Life and the Life-Giver.[15]

15. Jn 1:4, 6:63. See also *Ethical Discourse* 10.136; SCh 129:286.

So, then, profess with me that the Father engenders without pre-existing, that the Son is not engendered some time afterwards or as coming into being, and that the Holy Spirit proceeds but yet remains, with the Son, co-eternal and co-essential with the Father himself. Worship the whole Spirit in the whole Father, one and unoriginate, the whole Father in the whole Son, one and co-eternal, and the whole Son entire in the One Father and Spirit. [Worship] the one essence and nature in three persons, co-eternal, co-essential, without division or confusion, conceived as one sole principle of all things, the one God who created the universe. By means of things which touch upon you, you have been initiated into things which transcend you, so keep in mind that image with which |God| has honored you. Reason exists entire in that entire intelligence which you possess, and yet the soul is in both without any division or separation. This is what constitutes the image, that treasure we have received from on high; it is to be made in the likeness of God the Father and to bear the image of him who has begotten and created us. Thus, when we meet someone, even though he has intelligence, soul, and reason, we nonetheless pay him a single honor. We do not make distinctions or give preference to any of the three parts, but treat the man who has all three as undivided and unconfused. Because of this image of the Creator which we all share, we address and revere but one single man, not three distinct beings.

I beg you, then, |to reason| from the qualities you yourself bear and to think in this way about those of God who gave them to you, and worship the holy Trinity religiously as one single God, co-essential and without beginning in his oneness. Think of the privileges with which God has blessed you,[16] creating you in his own image and honoring you with this participation in his own properties. We profess that the Father is equal in glory to the Son and the Spirit and has the

16. Cf. 1 Jn 3:1.

same essence and the same power. The holy Trinity is one principle, authority, and dominion, just as you know that in us the intelligence is of equal glory to the reason and the soul, and is of the same glory and the same essence. Indeed they are all of one essence and nature. Because of our glory, and because of the fact that we have our being from God in being begotten and created by him, we are able to recognize and venerate God as our Father and Maker. If a man lacks one of these three, he cannot be a man. If we take away intelligence, then reason would be taken away with it, and he would be both senseless and irrational; if the soul [were taken away], intelligence and reason would be removed with it. Even if it were only a question of the immanent reason [being removed], then the whole living being would still be made useless, for an intelligence that cannot produce speech is unable to receive speech from someone else. How could it, being so mutilated and disordered in its true nature? It is just like breathing in air. The latter comes to us naturally, but if we are deprived of it, we collapse immediately; and in just the same way, intelligence has within itself by nature the rational faculty, and can certainly express it in speech. If, then, it is deprived of its natural ability to communicate and becomes separated and cut off from the immanent reason, then it perishes and is no longer of the slightest use.

⸀ To make my discussion of this bodily analogy more clear, I will consider childbirth as a simile for reason. If a woman has conceived a child, and does not deliver him into the world at the time appointed by nature, both she and her child will be in danger of death. In the same way, God has given our intelligence the natural property of constantly engendering speech, which is inseparable from it and inherent in its very essence. If you suppress this, you also suppress that which engendered it.

Now, if you are ready, turn your thoughts to the prototype and know without doubt that whoever denies the Son of God also denies the one who engendered him. And if he denies the Father and the Son, how can he fail, even in spite of himself, to deny the Spirit, too? If any man says that one of the persons is inferior or superior to the others, it only shows that he has not yet allowed the head of reason to rise up from the pit of the passions. Otherwise, he would be able to use the eyes of his mind to know himself truly and learn what this implies. The intelligence is not greater than the soul, nor the soul than the intelligence. Neither is the reason superior or inferior to either of them. In the same way there is no superiority or inferiority involved between the Father and the Son, or the Son in relation to the Father, or the Spirit in relation to both. They are at once without origin, and of the same glory and equal in dignity. Such conceptions as these are in no way applicable to the holy and equally glorious Trinity. So then, I ask you to think of transcendent matters from the analogy of your own experience, in accordance with the things which mark you out as the image of God.

It is a good thing to keep returning over and over again to this same point so that your senses may be illumined and you may gain a perfect understanding of the mysteries of the kingdom hidden within you. You are established in a dignity beyond all other creatures by being honored with reason, and by virtue of this, you rule over them all as king. Well then, as human intelligence | knows| itself by means of reason, and as the soul knows itself through both, in the same way we faithful have known, and still do know, God the Father through his only Son, his Word, and we know the Holy Spirit by the Father and the co-eternal Son. When the intelligence gives birth to the word, then the will of the soul has made itself known, either by the living voice or in writing, to those that hear it, and it is something that is common to both | parts|. It is obvious that they are not confused or split up into three, but instead one sees or conceives the three together in each one, in one single essence and one single will.

Analogously, in the case of the holy, co-essential, and indivisible Trinity, you must think and profess it with piety in this manner: the Father ineffably engenders God the Word whom he had within him in the beginning,[17] and he keeps him engendered without being separated, and high above all [spoken] word. The Son is generated eternally and inseparably from the Father who generates him without ever being separated from him. The Holy Spirit proceeds from the Father with the self-same nature as the co-essential Father and Son. He is united with them and is worshipped and glorified with them by all living things. But in all of them, you must recognize only one and the same will. All those who have been illumined from on high, even I in my lowliness, know that this is so. It has been revealed to us in the Holy Spirit by the grace of the Father through the Son.

Let us come again to the same point by a different road. This time we shall consecrate the example of our memory and speech. In the [divine persons], the super-essential essence of the one Godhead and dominion is in three hypostases. Since you believe this, you should confess with me clearly and without reservation that the three hypostases are united by nature, and are neither merged in a confusion nor split up into three. In fact, in each of them our intelligence can recognize the other two because there is but one essence, one nature, one single honor and will. Believe, then, that they are one God, who is the author and maker of all things visible and invisible.

If any man believes that God is the maker of all beings and has drawn them all from non-being, whether they be in heaven, on earth, or under the earth, then such a man, himself created by God, remains within his proper limits in knowing his Maker. He is drawn towards his Creator by the beauty of his creatures,[18] and praises and glorifies him as the Creator of all. Such a man will refrain from prying into his incom-

17. Jn 1:2.   18. Wis 13:5, Rom 1:20.

prehensible nature, for he knows, as I have said, that like all other things, he is simply a creature, whereas [God] is the maker of the universe, uncreated, without origin, incomprehensible, inexpressible, unfathomable, existing and pre-existing eternally. There was never a time when God was not, for he made all the ages and existed before any beginning. No one, therefore, can speculate about his beginning or discover his end. He was without origin. He is the principle of the universe and will exist eternally for infinite ages unlimited. He is the Inaccessible, the Invisible, the Inexpressible, the Ineffable, the One who cannot be comprehended by any of those he has made.

In times past we were earthly and base. We were deceived about many gods and worshipped the creation and venerated idols.[19] Then it was that he remained unknown to us. But he took pity on our ignorance and stooped down to our weakness, so that we might know that God is a perfect trinity in Father, Son, and Holy Spirit, and that he should be adored with piety. But as to his essence or his form, or where he is, or how great, or how he shares his essence, or the manner in which it is united — these are things which are never given to man to understand. Indeed, not even the Powers above have access to the inaccessibility of his super-essential essence. So do not try to quote me theological explanations drawn from the holy Scriptures, for these were given by the theologians against the blasphemous arguments of the heretics. You must understand that because the divine nature is inaccessible, it is also inconceivable, and what is inconceivable is altogether inexpressible. Is it not true that when we think about something and try to put it into words we are often totally unable to express it? Who, then, among men or angels would be able to explain the Invisible and the Inconceivable? For this is what all the Scriptures witness about him, and it was he who inspired them.

19. Cf. Rom 1:25.

No one at all could ever explain in words something which transcends being. It is impossible for the human spirit to conceive it. All the divine Scripture, through all the different ideas and expressions it applies to God, reveals to us that he is, not who he is.[20] Its witness teaches us only that he is eternally, and that he is who he is:[21] God the everlasting, three-personed, omnipotent, ruling all and seeing all, the maker and creator of all, beyond all need, wholly transcendent. We can know such a God only in the manner of a man who stands at night on the sands and holds out a lighted lantern to peer at the boundless immensity of the ocean's waves. How much of the whole limitless ocean do you think he could possibly see? Very little, if anything at all![22] But even if he cannot say how far it extends, he still sees the nature of the water quite distinctly, and here he makes no mistake. He knows well enough that what he is looking at is the sea, a fathomless ocean beyond his ability to view completely. So even though he does not see it, he still seems to perceive it in some way, for from that small part he does see, he forms an idea of the infinity of the waters.

If you like, we can take an indirect example to help us understand. Imagine we found a blind man who had never seen a spring of water and did not know what water was, because it was outside his experience and he had never tasted it. |Suppose| you described the natural properties of water to him: you tell him that it is beautiful, that it takes the form of lakes, wells, and even seas fed by rivers. Then he asks you about its nature, its appearance, its quality, and even its quantity; how it moves, where it comes from in the first place, how it spreads everywhere without running out—how would you answer these questions of his? For myself, I think that even if you had the most penetrating and speculative intellect you would not have the words to explain its origin, its es-

20. Cf. Basil the Great, *Adversus Eunomium* 1:14; PG 29:545.
21. Ex 3:14.   22. Cf. *Chapters* 2:11-14.

sence, or its movement. You would certainly be unable to teach him about its quality or quantity. How could you [explain it] to a man who had never seen or used the substance? But if words and explanations fail us with regard to something fluid, something that can be seen and touched, and we cannot answer those who ask us about its nature, origin, or composition, how could even one of the angels, or all of the saints together, possibly teach anything about the things of God and what concerns him to those who are ignorant of them? [How could they] teach about his essence and glory, or the nature of him who gave being to this universe? No one could ever do this. But as for the man who has been judged worthy to see God in the inaccessible glory of his divine and boundless light, even in the limited manner we have spoken of, such a man will have no need of any other teaching.[23] He has the entire [divinity] abiding within himself, and it moves him, speaks to him, and initiates him mystically into its hidden mysteries. This is in accordance with the divine word he gave: 'My mystery is for me and for mine.'[24] The only way to arrive at this contemplation is through the faithful observance of his precepts, provided that their observance is not spoiled by any kind of alteration through negligence or contempt, but kept and practised with fervent care. As a consequence, 'All those who shall keep to this rule[25] will not find themselves far from the kingdom of heaven.'[26] In proportion to their fervor and their zealous joy in this observance, then sooner or later, in a greater or lesser degree, they will earn the reward of the vision of God and become participants in the divine nature.[27] They will be called gods through adoption, and sons of God in Jesus Christ our Lord, to whom be glory and dominion with the Father and the all-holy Spirit, now and forever, and through the ages of ages. Amen.

23. Cf. Jer 31:34, 1 Jn 2:27.
24. Cited in *Theological Discourse* 1. See also Nicetas Stethatos, *Opuscules et lettres*; SCh 81:280.
25. Gal 6:16.   26. Mk 12:34.   27. 2 Pet 1:4.

THE THIRD THEOLOGICAL DISCOURSE

THAT IF THE FATHER IS ONE THING, THEN SO TOO IS THE
SON; AND IF THE SON IS SUCH, THEN SO TOO IS THE SPIRIT.
THAT THE THREE ARE ONE SPIRIT OF THE SAME
GLORY, ESSENCE, AND THRONE.

GOD IS ALWAYS ONE. He is always called the one God. We name him as such in our hymns and doxologies: the eternal Father, the co-eternal Son of the Father, and the all-holy Spirit, co-eternal and co-essential with the Father and the Son. This is the co-essential Trinity which is one nature, glory, and origin. This is the one principle of all, the one power, royalty, and omnipotent sovereignty which gives existence to all and creates all from the same throne and in the same glory. When we consider the unity in faith, we worship God as one, and when we profess our faith in the Trinity, we offer praise to the Trinity in the distinct hypostases. This is just as our Lord Jesus Christ has initiated us. He who is one of the three-personed Godhead told us to baptize in the name of the Father and the Son and the Holy Spirit.[1] On another occasion he said: 'My Father is greater than I.'[2] This was to show that he is distinct from the Father. And again: 'I do nothing of myself.'[3] And yet again: 'I shall ask the Father[4] and he will send you another comforter, the Spirit of truth which proceeds from the Father.'[5] In this way, he called the Spirit 'another.'

It is grace, then, that allows us to understand the absolute unity of Godhead and Dominion in three co-essential hypos-

1. Mt 28:19.   3. Jn 8:28.   5. Jn 15:26.
2. Jn 14:28.   4. Jn 14:16.

[134]

tases, as well as the permanent identity of the three hypostases within the eternal glory and the inseparable Oneness. We know that whenever God the Son is wholly named then the Father is wholly present with the Spirit; that when God the Father is wholly praised the Son is wholly there through the Spirit; and that when the Father is wholly confessed and glorified with the Son, then there too is the whole Spirit. This is the mystery which the Spirit teaches us: that the persons are in this way identical in essence and glory, or in other words, the hypostases are united without division or confusion within their one divine nature as the creative cause of all being. Thus, whenever the working of the Spirit lifts us up with him to God the Father through the Son, we stretch out our hands and raise our eyes to him, and say: 'Our Father who are in heaven.'[6] Then in that Spirit which confers the understanding, we approach the only Son of the Father to present our prayers to him, and here we say: 'Only Son, co-eternal Word of God the Father, the only one of the only one, God from God, one without beginning from him who has no beginning, eternal from the eternal, everlasting from everlasting, light from light, life from life, inaccessible from the inaccessible, inconceivable from the inconceivable, inexpressible from the inexpressible, immutable from the immutable, incomprehensible from the incomprehensible, forgive us our sins.' In the same way we invoke the Holy Spirit by saying this: 'Holy Spirit, |you| who proceed ineffably from the Father and live in us faithful through the Son, spirit of life and understanding, spirit of holiness and perfection, good spirit and wise, friend of man, gentle and glorious one who refreshes us with food and drink, all merciful giver of light and strength, divine spirit of patience, spirit who gives us joy and gladness, temperance, wisdom, knowledge, and sweetness, you make us forget all our injuries and cares here below, and |bestow upon us| the vision of the good things above.

6. Mt 6:9.

You drive off indolence and take away negligence, putting our curiosity and malice to flight. Spirit, revealer of mysteries, pledge of the kingdom of heaven, source of prophecy, vessel of instruction, remedy of sin and gateway of all repentance, you are like the gatekeeper who shows the way to all who are searching. Spirit of love, peace, faith, and moderation, spirit of desire inspiring desire, come and live in us and stay undivided and inseparable within us. Sanctify our hearts, transform and illumine them, you who are of the same essence and glory as the Son and the Father. You make gods of all who welcome you, wiping out every sin and bringing every virtue with your incoming. You do not have to look beyond yourself to meet all our needs, for you yourself are the substance of all that is good, and those in whom you come to dwell have in their hearts the essence of all good.

We do not offer our hymn, then, to three gods instead of one, as if we were dividing the indissoluble unity of the whole. No, we worship the Son and the Spirit in the Father, the Spirit and the Father in the son, and the Father and the Son in the Spirit. We glorify them as one nature of one Godhead in three persons, of the same power and the same essence, self-determinant, all powerful, self-willing, co-eternal, without origin, super-essential, and without confusion or division. We do not imagine that there is one being, then another, and yet a third, one being of such a nature and the others of different kinds, for this would be to divide the oneness of the indivisible Godhead and stupidly introduce alien distinctions into his nature. On the contrary, we know the three as one single God, indivisibly divided into the hypostases and united without confusion in the oneness of a single essence. He is wholly one in the hypostases and wholly threefold in the super-essential unity. We must call the same God three in the persons and one in the unity of essence or nature.

It is in this way that the only Son of the Father has showed all of us quite clearly that in all things he is of the same glory, essence, and dominion as the co-essential Father and Spirit, for he says, 'I and the Father are one.'[7] And at another time, he showed that the Spirit came forth without any change from this essence when he said: 'The Spirit of truth proceeds from the Father.'[8] Just as the waters of a river come from an 'eye', that is, a spring of water, so too God the Spirit proceeds from God the Father. And this is why he also said: 'God is Spirit and those who worship him must worship in spirit and in truth.'[9] If, then, the Father is Spirit, it is evident that the Son born from him must equally be Spirit.'[10] And if he assumed flesh, he rendered it divine and spiritual. The Holy Spirit is Spirit, for he proceeds from the Father and is given through the Son to us, unworthy though we are. It is not to say that he is sent out or distributed against his will, for in fact, through another in the Trinity, the Son himself, he is fulfilling his own will, which is the good-will of the Father. The Holy Trinity is indivisible in its nature, essence, and will, but because it is | three | hypostases it receives the personal names of Father, Son, and Holy Spirit. Yet there is one God whose name is Trinity, and since he is above every name that can be named[11] and beyond all word or expression, he is transcendent; and since he is no | particularized | thing, he goes beyond the scope of all comprehension.

So, then, understand how the holy Scripture says that the three are one. It is good to take up this same | point | and continue speaking on these things, for the man who knows how to delight in them in a manner pleasing to God finds here a constant source of joy, and the divine word sanctifies the feelings of his soul. It is said: 'God is Spirit', and as we have said, the Son too must be | Spirit |. So if God is Spirit and the Lord is the Spirit, and if the divine Scriptures call the Lord 'Spirit', then it follows that God is one Spirit known

7. Jn 10:30.   9. Jn 4:24.   11. Eph 1:21.
8. Jn 15:26.   10. 2 Cor 3:17.

in three persons or hypostases. This was why the Son spoke of the 'One,'[12] in order to make us understand. But in all there is the same power, the same throne, the same nature, and the same essence. If the persons are called one single Spirit in this way, it is in order that you should not suppose that there is any inequality in the three persons of the Trinity, no superiority or inferiority. There is no division of any sort that can be rightly applied. The names do not signify this, but are there as a means of teaching us of the very existence of the hypostases and persons. If we are so taught and sufficiently initiated in the affairs of God, we should not be so indiscreet as to inquire any further. By faith we receive this much alone. Keep to it, be assured, and profess that the things above us are completely beyond our comprehension.

However, we will initiate you into this fact as well: that God is light,[13] a light infinite and incomprehensible,[14] for then you will know about the properties of the divine nature, how God and all that is of God, from God, and within God, is one light, worshipped in each of the hypostases and perceived in all the qualities and gifts of God. Everything to do with God is light, and [this light] is common to all the persons, divided between them indivisibly. But if for your sake I may speak of the indivisible as if it were divided: the Father is light, the Son is light, the Holy Spirit is light; one single light as they are simple, non-composite, timeless, eternal, and possessed of the same honor and glory. All that comes from him is light, and is given to us as arising from the light. The light is life. The light is immortality. The light is the source of life. The light is living water, charity, peace, truth, and the door of the kingdom of heaven. The light is the very kingdom itself. The light is the bridal chamber, the bridal couch, paradise, and all the bliss of paradise. It is the land of the gentle, the crowns of life, and the very garments of the

12. Jn 10:30, 17:22.   13. 1 Jn 1:5.
14. Cf. Gregory Nazianzen, *Orationes* 31.3; PG 36:136.

saints. The light is Jesus Christ, the Saviour and King of the universe. The bread of his sinless flesh is light. The chalice of his precious blood is light. His resurrection is light. His face is light. His hand, his finger, his mouth, his eyes, all are light. The Lord is light, and his voice is as light from light. Light is the comforter, the pearl, the seed of mustard, the true vine, the leaven, hope, and faith — all are light.[15]

So all this and everything else you might hear from the apostles and prophets about the inexpressible and super-essential deity you must understand, I beg you, as being by essence the one principle which is above all principles, adored in the unity of the threefold light. For God is one in Father, Son, and Holy Spirit. He is light inaccessible, pre-existing the ages. He bears all these titles and can be designated by all such terms we use and many others besides. And these are not just names, but energies. I have been taught this by men who have learned it from their own experience, men who have been securely taught about the good things inherent in the infinitely good God from their own contemplation. Indeed, I will show you in passing some of the other 'lights' applicable to God: his goodness is light; his compassion is light; his mercy, his embrace, his watchful care are light. His sceptre is light, his crook, and his consolation.[16]

Now the majority of these terms, in fact all of them, can be applied to us, but then they apply only in a human way. To him they apply as God. Nor will I hesitate in repeating them for you one by one: God is called Father, and most men are called fathers, too. The divine Christ is the Son of God, and so too are we sons of men. The all-holy Spirit is the Spirit of God, and our souls, too, are called spirit. God is life, and we too are said to be alive. God is love, and mutual love exists even between great sinners. But does this mean that we equate God with human love? No, this is blasphemy! Could

15. Cf. Mt 13:46, 17:20, Lk 17:6, Jn 15:1, 5, Gal 5:9, 1 Co 13:13.
16. Ps 23:4.

we even claim that the peace we men experience is 'that peace which passes all understanding'?[17] Of course not, for the peace we know is usually a matter of avoiding disputes and wrangles. Then does God's truth simply amount to the fact that he does not lie to anyone? Again, not at all. The words of men are ephemeral and pass away, but the word of God is something alive and real and active.[18] It is, in fact, true God, God and truth itself. It transcends all human thought and speech. It is unchangeable, unalterable, subsisting in its own life. And likewise the water which we see is not that 'living water',[19] nor is our bread like that 'living bread';[20] no, as I have said previously, all these things are light, and God is the one single light. The man who shares in this thereby shares in all the good things we have spoken about, in both senses. Such a man becomes gentle and humble, for these things, along with all the rest, are also light. In short, the man who has this light has, with this light, all other things as well. In addition to all this, God could also be called the Watchman,[21] for when he enters to live in a man, he wakens up his soul to the good, and for that soul he becomes every good. And when it has God indwelling, it lacks no good thing,[22] but is always full to overflowing[23] with all the breath-taking gifts of God. It is at home with the ranks of heavenly powers and shares in their joy. Let all of us, then, strive to win and enjoy these riches by the grace and kindness of our Lord Jesus Christ, to whom be glory and dominion with the Father and the Holy Spirit, now and forever, and through the ages of ages. Amen.

17. Phil 4:7.   20. Jn 7:38.   23. Ps 23:5.
18. Heb 4:12.   21. Jer 1:12.
19. Jn 6:51.   22. Ps 34:11.

ABBREVIATIONS

DTC   *Dictionnaire de Théologie Catholique*, ed. E. Amann.
      Paris. (1899). 1903-50.

PG   J. P. Migne, *Patrologia Graeca*. Paris. 1857-66.

SB   *Supplementum Byzantinum.*

SCh   *Sources chrétiennes.* Paris, 1941-.

BIBLIOGRAPHY

EDITIONS OF THE WORKS

J. P. Migne. *Opera Symeonis Junioris. Patrologia cursus completus, series graeca* (PG) 120. He follows the Latin Edition of Jacobus Pontanus, (Ingolstadt, 1603) and sometimes the Greek version from the *Philocalia*, (Edd. Nicodemus of Agioritis and Makarios of Corinth. Venice, 1782) listing the following:

Orationes 33. PG 120:321-507.

Divinorum amorum liber singularis. PG 120:507.

Capita practica et theologica. PG 120:604.

(*De alterationibus animae et corporis*)
De fide et profectu libellus. PG 120:693.

De tribus modis orationis. PG 120:701.

(*Dialogus scholasticis cujusdam de Deo ad Symeonem*.)

Symeon's *Epistola de confessione* is misattributed to John of Damascus in PG 95.

J. Darrouzès. *Chapitres théologiques, gnostiques et pratiques. Sources Chrétiennes* (SCh), vol. 51. Paris, 1957.

———. *Traités théologiques et éthiques*. SCh 122, 129. Paris, 1966-7.

B. Krivocheine. *Catéchèses*. SCh 96, 104 and 113. Paris, 1963-5. (Vol. 113 contains the text of the *Eucharistic prayers*.)

J. Koder. *Hymnes*. SCh 156, 174. Paris, 1969.

A. Kambylis. *Hymnen. Symeon Neos Theologos. Suppl. Byzantinum*. No. 3. Berlin/New York, 1976.

G. Maloney, trans. *Hymns of Divine Love*. Denville, New Jersey, 1976.

K. Kirchhoff. *Symeon der Neue Theologe. Licht vom Licht*. 1930, 1951.

Orthodox Theological Texts. *The Sin of Adam and Our Redemption: Seven homilies of St. Symeon*. Platina, California, 1979.

STUDIES

L. Allatius. *De Symeonum scriptis diatriba.* Paris, 1664. (cf. PG 120:287ff.)

B. Altaner. *Patrology.* London, 1960.

O. Bardenhewer. *Patrology.* St. Louis, 1908.

H. G. Beck. *Kirche und theologische Literatur im byzantinischen Reich.* Munich, 1959, cp. pp. 360-2.

J. Bois. 'Les Hésychastes avant le xive siècle.' *Echos d'Orient,* 5 (1901).

A. Ehrhard, Ed. *Geschichte der byzantinischen Literatur.* Munich, 1897. See pp. 154ff.

A. Ehrhard. *Byzantinische Zeitschrift,* 33. 1933, pp. 380ff.

Fabricus. *Bibliotheca Graeca,* 10. Hamburg, 1737, pp. 299ff.

J. Gouillard. 'Symeon le Jeune.' *Dictionnaire de Théologie Catholique,* 14, pt. 2. Paris, 1941, cols. 2941-2959.

Fr. Halkin. *Analecta Bollandiana,* 48, p. 201.

I. Hausherr, ⎱ *Un grand Byzantin mystique. Vie de S. Sy-* G. Horn, (eds) ⎰ *méon le Nouveau Théologien par Nicetas Stethatos. Orientalia Christinana,* 12, no. 45. Rome, 1928.

I. Hausherr. *La méthode d'oraison hésychaste. Orientalia Christiana* 9, 2, no. 36. Rome, 1927.

K. Holl. *Enthusiasmus und Bussegewalt beim griechischen Mönchtum. Eine Studie zu Symeon dem neuen Theologen.* Leipzig, 1898.

K. Holl. 'Symeon der Neue Theologe.' *Prot. Realencyclopädie,* (3rd Edn.) 19. 1903, pp. 215-219.

———. *Gessammelte Aufsätze zur Kirchengeschichte,* 2. 1928, pp. 403-410.

J. M. Hussey. *Church and Learning in the Byzantine Empire.* London, 1937, pp. 201ff.

M. Jugie. 'La méthode d'oraison hésychaste.' *Echos d'Orient,* 30 (1931).

H. Koch. *Historisches Jahrbuch.* 1900, pp. 58f.

B. Krivocheine. '*The brother loving poor man.* The mystical autobiography of S. Symeon the New Theologian.' *Christian East*, NS, 2 (1953-4).

———. *The writings of S. Symeon the New Theologian. Orientalis Christiana Periodica*, 201. Rome, 1954, pp. 298-328.

———. 'The most enthusiastic zealot.' *Ostkirchliche Studien*, 4 1955, pp. 108-128.

———. *Dans la lumière du Christ.* Chevetògne. 1980.

F. Lascaris. 'The liberation of Man in Symeon the New Theologian.' Diss. Oxford, 1969.

V. Laurent. 'Un nouveau monument hagiographique.' *Echos d'Orient*, 27. 1928, pp. 431f.

M. Lot-Borodine. 'La doctrine de déification dans l'église grecque jusqu'au 11ᵉ siècle.' *Revue d'histoire des Religions*, 105 (1932) pp. 5ff; vol. 106 (1932) 515ff; vol. 107 (1933) 8ff.

———. 'Le mystère du don des larmes dans l'Orient Chrétien.' *Vie Spirituelle*, 48, pp. 65f.

G. Maloney. *The Mystic of Fire and Love.* Denville, New Jersey, 1975.

———. *Russian Hesychasm.* The Hague, 1973.

J. Meyendorff. *Introduction à l'étude de Grégoire Palamas. Patristica Sorbonensa*, 3. Paris, 1959.

P. Miguel. 'La conscience de la grace selon Symeon le Nouveau Théologien.' *Irénikon* 43. 1969, pp. 314-42.

L. Petit. 'La vie et œuvre de Symeon le Nouveau Théologien.' *Echos d'Orient*, 27. 1928, pp. 163f.

———. *Bibliothèque des acolouthies Grecques.* Brussels, 1926. See pp. 270f.

D. Scholarios. *Kleis Patrologias.* Athens, 1879, pp. 496.

W. Völker. *Praxis und theoria bei Symeon dem Neuen Theologen. Ein Beitrag zur byzantinischen Mystik.* 1974.

———. *Scala Paradisi: Eine Studie zu Johannes Climacus und zugleich eine Vorstudie zu Symeon dem Neuen Theologen.* Wiesbaden, 1968.

CISTERCIAN PUBLICATIONS INC.

TITLES LISTING

THE CISTERCIAN FATHERS SERIES

THE CISTERCIAN STUDIES SERIES

Temporarily out of print   †Forthcoming

~rigorist~

Not much on
      – Divine Office   3.100 – continuous prayer
      – Sacraments   3.45 – baptism